THE BIKE BOOK

THE BIKE BOOK

Editor
TIM HUGHES

GALLERY BOOKS
An Imprint of W. H. Smith Publishers Inc.
112 Madison Avenue
New York City 10016

Copyright © Sackville Design Group Ltd 1990
Text © Tim Hughes, Nick Hamlyn and Robert Garbutt 1990
This book was designed and produced by
Sackville Design Group Ltd
Hales Barn, Stradbroke, Suffolk IP21 5JG

Designer: Al Rockall
Editor: Mike Henderson
Production: Ruth Nicolas

This edition first published in the United States in 1990 by Gallery Books,
an imprint of W.H. Smith Publishers Inc.,
112 Madison Avenue, New York, New York 10016

Gallery Books are available for bulk purchase for sales promotions and premium use.
For details write or telephone the Manager of Special Sales, W.H. Smith Publishers, Inc.,
112 Madison Avenue, New York, New York 10016. (212) 532-6600

Printed and bound in Holland by Rotosmeets, Weert

Contents

6

Bicycles and using them

Introduction

If you've just picked up *The Bike Book*, the chances are that you have been thinking about cycling as a leisure pastime or sport, for that's what the book is about. The scope of cycling as a sport is enormous. At one end of the scale there is the beginner dabbling in a club race or time-trial, at the other the professional taking in three or four Alpine passes in a day on the way to victory in the Tour de France, or whirling through the winter on the steep wooden bankings of the six-day race tracks. In between there are amateur races from a few hundred metres to hundreds of miles or kilometres, or time-trials from 10 miles (16 km) to 24 hours.

But many cyclists aren't competitively inclined at all. For them the bicycle is a passport to travel, a very special personal and silent travel. There aren't many pastimes which combine a pleasant, rhythmic and healthy 'green' exercise with the chance to explore the roads – and beyond the roads – of the world. For them it's not necessarily the distances covered, nor a chronicle of hours, minutes and seconds, but an accumulation of sights, sounds, scents and new experiences.

Meanwhile, it's worth remembering that cycling is far more than a mere sport (and even to some sporting cyclists it seems nearer to a religion). For millions of people, in Africa, in Asia and in many parts of Europe, it is an essential form of transport, serving in every role from pack-donkey upwards. In every country of the developing world some form of bicycle is

(Opposite) Descending into the valley of the Eyrieux near Les Ollières in the Ardèches, France. This is ideal cycling country. (Left) The Scottish border country (here near Hawkshaw, Tweeddale) is sometimes overlooked by cyclists who head further north.

coupled to mobile shops, to travelling workshops, to every form of enterprise.

Even in the developed countries of north America and Europe, there seem, at a first glance, to be hundreds of different types of bicycle. There are sleek racing bikes with dropped handlebars and narrow tyres(US: tires); there are sedate, matronly roadsters; there are aggressively knobbly-tyred mountainbikes; there are demure equipped-to-go-anywhere tourers; there are tandems and tricycles; there are bikes for children, for women, for everybody. There are bicycles for travelling almost any distance you choose, how you like.

Yet all these bicycles have their ultimate origins in the 'dandy'- or 'hobby-horse' (or célérifère) of the early nineteenth century. By about 1820, one of its pioneers, Baron von Drais de Sauerbrun, was putting it to practical use on his estates and his version became known as the draisienne. The machine was at least recognizably a bicycle in that it had two equal-sized wooden wheels mounted in iron forks, the rear rigidly held and the front one capable of being steered by a handle. There were no pedals, though. To propel it, the rider sat astride the stout wooden 'perch' that linked the two wheel-forks, with a cushion the only concession to comfort, and paddled the contraption along 'by running with long and forcible strides, the machine of course progressing between the strokes and of its own accord downhill', in the words of a near-contemporary chronicler. However, the account continues, 'riders were unmercifully lampooned and ridiculed, and the peculiarly awkward position (which tended to produce hernia) soon obtained for the machine a very bad name.'

The notion of attaching some form of crank and pedal to one of the wheels seems to have occurred independently to several people over the next twenty years or so – and in any case cranked handles for driving machinery, and indeed cranks and pistons, were already commonplace. Applying cranks to bicycles brought with it a dilemma: should they be fitted to the front wheel or the rear? Both were in fact tried, leading to two distinct lines of development, one of them ultimately a dead end.

In Britain at least, credit for first fitting cranks of a kind is accorded on documentary evidence to a Scot, Kirkpatrick Macmillan, a Dumfriesshire blacksmith, somewhere around 1840. Ahead of his time, Macmillan chose to drive the rear wheel through a treadle arrangement, anticipating modern rear-wheel drive bicycles – which were not to be re-invented for nearly another forty years.

Meanwhile, in France, the inventive Michaux family developed around 1861 a pedal-driven version of the hobby-horse, by fitting cranks to the *front* wheel. The design of their *vélocipède*, as they termed it, was soon refined and copied world-wide. The distance travelled for each

(Right) The lofty elegance of the Ordinary or 'Penny Farthing'. On these bikes steep descents were treated with caution. (Above) An early bicycle made for two — more sociable perhaps than the modern tandem.

(Left) An egg and spoon race on bicycles dating from the early 1900s. Note the man's drop handlebars. (Below) A military formation for resisting cavalry attack in 1889. Eccentric as it may seem, the spinning wheels were said to frighten the horses. The bikes were not seriously meant as a barricade.

pedal stroke was dependent entirely on the diameter of the front wheel. As designs improved, with easier-running bearings, tubular frame and fork construction, and rubber-tyred wheels, so the size of the front wheel began to increase to give higher effective gearing, until in the apotheosis of the High Ordinary Bicycle it reached the limits its rider could straddle.

Sadly, the lofty elegance of the Ordinary was doomed, and after flowering into the mid-1880s, with devotees staying with it almost to the end of the century, a radical new design took over. It was the end of the line for the front-wheel drive. By then, nevertheless, Ordinary riders had put in some prodigious performances, probably the most noteworthy G.P. Mills' 1886 Land's End to John o'Groats ride in 5 days 1 hr 45 min on a machine with a 53-in front wheel. The distance was 861 miles (1395 km) and many of the roads must have been what we would consider rough tracks today. He followed it up later in the same year with a 5 day 10 hr ride on a tricycle.

Towards the end of the 1870s the beginnings of today's bicycles became apparent. Although he was not the first to devise a rear-driven bicycle with smallish equally-sized wheels, cranks and a chain, J.K. Starley's Rover of 1885 is generally credited as the first really commercially successful design. (The design was so seminal that in several slavonic languages a version of 'rover' is the modern word for bicycle!) The Rover had all the features of a modern bicycle except the final triangulating frame seat tube. By making the pedal-driven chainwheel larger than that on the wheel hub, gearing could be freed from wheel size. The great advantage, though, was the ease of mounting and the low centre of gravity, leading to greater stability. The name 'safety bicycle' was soon coined. Dunlop's pneumatic tyre rapidly followed, in 1888, and the stage was set for the gradual development of the modern bicycle.

Modern bicycle frames may be more compact, their wheels a little smaller and closer together, while new materials that Starley never knew (aluminium alloys – a semi-precious metal in his time!, high-strength alloy steels, plastics, carbon fibres) find a place in today's machines – but most of their features stem from that fertile time and the Victorian genius for invention.

From the same time, too, comes most of the foundations of present-day cycling activity. The first bicycle track race was held in France in 1868 and the first in Britain the following year. Also in 1869, the first road race – from Paris to Rouen – attracted over 200 riders, and the first cycling magazines were published in France and the USA. Bicycle clubs date from this time, too, and in 1878 two British national organisations, the Bicycle Touring Club and the National Cyclists' Union, were founded. (Both are still active as the CTC (Cyclists' Touring Club) and BCF (British Cycling Federation) respectively.) In 1880, the United States followed suit and the League of American Wheelmen was formed. The bicycle had obviously come to stay.

Cycle Sport. (Below) Phil Anderson, winner of several classic road races and a dynamic rider. (Right) Two world champions side by side. On the left is Irishman Sean Kelly and right is American Greg LeMond, winner of the 1989 Tour de France and the World Professional race.

(Left) Stephen Roche, only the second rider to win the Giro d'Italia, Tour de France and World Professional road race in the same year. (Centre) Time-trial specialist Ian Cammish, holder of two important records. (Top) A mountain bike racer. Mountain bike racing looks set to become a major branch of cycle sport. The USA already has a number of professional teams.

Types of bicycle

The anatomy of the bicycle

All bicycles have two wheels, a frame, handlebars, saddle, pedals, chainwheel, chain, and hub sprocket(s). And although the details may differ, the names of the main parts will remain the same.

Several design factors affect the handling and feel of the bicycle, accounting for the very different look of the different types. Light weight makes a bicycle easier to propel, so racing bicycles use light frames, components, and wheels and tyres. Very light components may not be so robust or long-lived, so other bicycles may use stouter fittings, particularly wheels and tyres. A racer may find that the potential rewards make it worth using exotic and highly expensive materials such as carbon fibre, which might be too costly for the ordinary rider. At the other extreme a mountain bike has to stand up to pounding over rough ground, so strength takes precedence over weight.

The actual shape of the bicycle frame and forks is important. A steeper frame, with more upright head and seat angles, with front forks more nearly straight and the wheelbase shorter, responds more rapidly to effort and accelerates faster. But steep frames and straighter forks absorb fewer road shocks and can feel twitchy. So touring bicycles and – even more – mountain bikes have shallower frame angles. The rolling resistance of narrow and above all thin tyres (US:tires) is less. The racer takes the risk and accepts the harder ride; tourers and mountain-bikers go for comfort and reliability.

At racing speeds wind resistance is most important: the work a rider has to do to overcome it increases with the cube of the speed – cutting through the air at 50 kph takes not twenty-five per cent more work than 40 kph, but ninety-five per cent. So, racing bikes and their riders do what they can to reduce wind-resistance, within the sometimes-confining rules of competition. And, as we shall see later, lessening wind resistance by riding in the shelter of another rider is the basis of all the complex tactics of road and track racing.

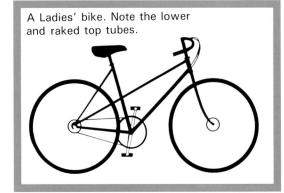

A Ladies' bike. Note the lower and raked top tubes.

top tube

saddle

seat pin or saddle stem

seat stays

seat tube

back brake

front derailleur

quick release

hub axle or spindle

hub

freewheel or block

rear derailleur

valve

chainstays

chainrings

crankset or chainwheel

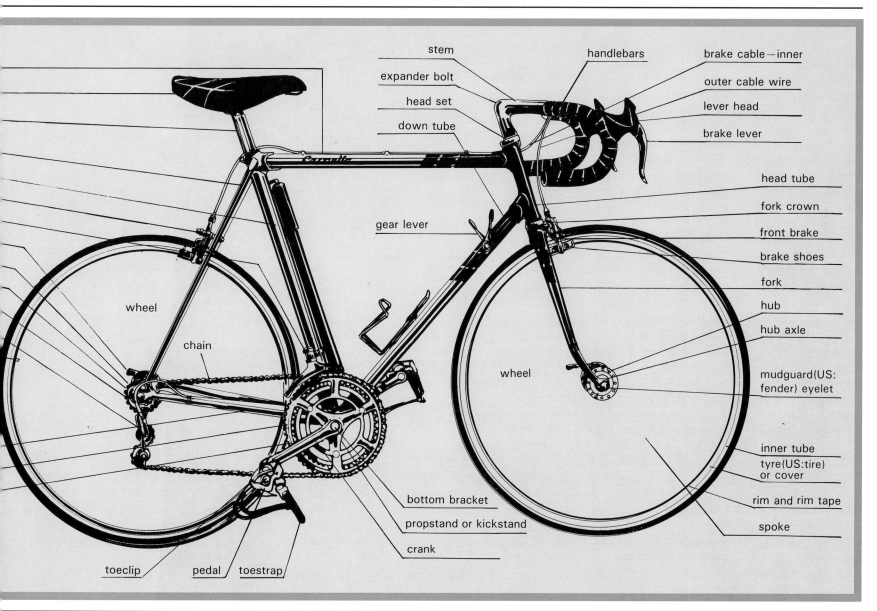

stem

expander bolt

head set

down tube

handlebars

brake cable—inner

outer cable wire

lever head

brake lever

gear lever

head tube

fork crown

front brake

brake shoes

fork

hub

hub axle

wheel

chain

wheel

mudguard(US: fender) eyelet

inner tube

tyre(US:tire) or cover

rim and rim tape

spoke

bottom bracket

propstand or kickstand

crank

toeclip

pedal

toestrap

Gear ratios

Another critical difference between different specialized bikes lies in the gear ratios fitted. As we saw in the introduction, the use of chain drive with different-sized chainwheels allowed the gear ratio – essentially a measure of the distance travelled for each turn of the pedals – to be independent of the wheel size. Habits die hard, though, and a hundred years later gear ratios are *still* often quoted in Britain and the USA as the size (in inches) of front wheel an old High Ordinary would have at the same gearing: a modern bike with a '53-inch' gear would go as far with each pedal turn as G.P. Mills' record-breaking Beeston Humber. There is a formula for calculating this number: it's *actual wheel diameter* (in inches) multiplied by the *number* of *teeth on the front* (pedal crank) *chainwheel* and then divided by the *number of teeth on the rear* (hub) *sprocket*. In other countries the *gear development* is used: this is the distance in metres travelled per complete pedal revolution. Often, though, it's simpler and less ambiguous to quote front chainwheel and rear sprocket sizes particularly when suggesting specifications (the conventional form is '48 × 18', for front and rear respectively).

The mechanics of gearing

Nowadays the overwhelming majority of variable gear systems use the derailleur system. Gear mechanisms shift the chain between two or three different-sized chainwheels at the front and a multiple freewheel (US: cluster) with five

A rear gear mechanism typical of most variable gear systems. In recent years the derailleur has been considerably refined.

A Sachs Pentasport hub gear, giving five speeds and a coaster brake in one hub. A recent advance in bike engineering.

to seven different-sized sprockets at the back, to give the different ratios. Since the readily available sizes of chainring run from 24 to 55 teeth and of rear sprocket from 12 to 34, the theoretically possible range is enormous – from 19 to 124 inches (1.5 to 10 metres development). The chain obviously has to be long enough to go round the largest chainwheel and the largest rear sprocket used, so rear gear mechanisms have a spring-loaded tension arm which takes up the slack at other times. Gear mechanisms have become very refined over the last few years and

one of the former obstacles to easy use of derailleur gears – that there were no definite shift lever positions for each gear – has been overcome. Virtually all rear gear mechanisms sold can be fitted up as 'indexed' systems, with click positions for each gear. Some front gears are also indexed. However, the chain will only derail from one sprocket or chainring to the next while you are pedalling; you can't change gear when freewheeling or stopped.

The concept of a chain that does not run in an exact fore-and-aft line is now generally

cassette hub with integral 2 speed

quick release hub

double chainset

frame-mounted gear levers

brake caliper

brake levers

front gear mechanism

rear gear mechanism

chain and freewheel

A Sachs Huret group set, featuring an Aris gear system. The chainset is forged in light alloy and silver anodized. The gear has a capacity for up to a 32 sprocket.

accepted and modern chains are designed to be used in this way. Nevertheless, in practice, it is customary to use the outermost chainring with the outer sprockets, the middle ring with the middle sprockets and the innermost with the inner ones. This means that although a combination of, say, three chainrings and six sprockets theoretically offers 18 different ratios, the actual practical number is about 12 to 14. In use, too, you don't usually keep switching both gear mechanisms to go up through every ratio in order. In passing, you should be warned that there are about as many different concepts of the ideal gearing range as there are cyclists.

The older and now much less common type of variable gear is an epicyclic system built into the rear hub. Those still on the market offer either three or five rather widely-spaced ratios. They have the advantages that the mechanism is sealed away from road dirt and that they can be changed when stationary. The disadvantages are that the total range is restricted and fixed (even though the ratios are too widely spaced for some tastes and purposes) and that when they do need servicing it is a quite skilled job. Once a virtual monopoly of the English Sturmey-Archer company there is now evidence of wider interest in hub gears in Europe and Japan and developments are possible. They are most commonly fitted to about-town and 'roadster' bikes.

Tyres(US:tires) and wheels

All tyres have two components: the outside visible part with the patterned tread and an inner airtight tube. In the most commonly used type the outer cover and the tube are separate components, and the U-shaped outer is located on the rim by steel or high-tensile plastic wires built into the tyre edges. These slip over the edge of the rim and seat on the inner side of it. This type is known as a wired-on tyre (US: 'clincher'). The advantage is that it can be relatively cheap and that the inner tube can be easily repaired or replaced if it is punctured. There are limits to how light or thin they can be made however, and while there are nowadays some quite light wired-on tyres available, the tubular tyre (US: 'sew-up') still holds sway for most top-quality racing. These tyres have the extremely delicate inner tube permanently located inside a tube-section outer which is sewn up along the base. The stitching is protected by a base tape which is secured to a special crescent-shaped rim by, usually, a rubber-based adhesive. A punctured tubular has to be removed and replaced by a spare, while mending them is a lengthy and tricky task. The advantages are entirely in their lightness and responsive feel, so they are used virtually exclusively for racing.

All but the cheapest wheels nowadays have aluminium alloy rims and hubs. Hubs are fixed into the frame in one of two ways; quick-release hubs have a cam-operated lever which locks the hub into position in one single motion, while solid-axle hubs are held in place by hexagonal

Special tyres are made for different uses. This cyclo-cross tyre has a tread for muddy conditions.

A disc wheel used in racing. Although extremely light in construction they are also expensive.

nuts with built-in serrated gripping washers ('track nuts'). Quick-release hubs were originally developed to allow rapid wheel changes in road races but they have a lot of advantages for normal touring wheels. Some mountain-bikes have quick-release hubs, too, although many have a combination of quick-release front wheel and solid-axle rear. It is of course necessary to use the appropriate spanner (US: wrench) to loosen/tighten the track nuts.

Wheel and tyre sizes can be bewildering. A lot of loose descriptions are used – for instance, there are no less than four '26-inch' sizes in fairly common use! There is now an agreed European (ETRTO) designation which is marked on the side of wired-on tyres and gives the nominal cross-section and fairly accurate bead seat diameter, both in mm. The corresponding bead seat diameter is now also to be marked on rims. Tyres are only compatible with rims of the correct bead seat diameter (the last figure of the third column in the table below) and also require one of the appropriate width, although there's some latitude in this. The following table for wired-on tyres gives the ETRTO equivalents of the commonest British/American and European colloquial designations. (Only a sample of the common widths in a particular diameter are quoted.) The standard-sized rim for tubular tyres is the same size as 700C, 622 mm.

A cross-section of a cycle tyre

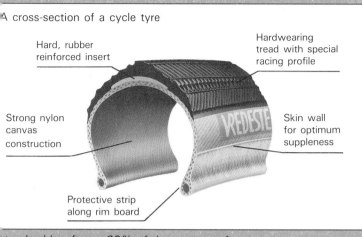

Hard, rubber reinforced insert

Hardwearing tread with special racing profile

Strong nylon canvas construction

Skin wall for optimum suppleness

Protective strip along rim board

natural rubber forms 60% of the content of
many tyres. It is mixed with synthetic rubber and
chemical additives and softened prior to use.

Common British/ American description	Common European designation	ETRTO marking
27×1	no equivalent	25-630
$27 \times 1\frac{1}{4}$	no equivalent	32-630
$700 \times 19C$	$700 \times 19C$	19-622
$700 \times 28C$	$700 \times 28C$	28-622
$700 \times 35C$	$700 \times 35C$	35-622
$26 \times 1\frac{1}{4}$	no equivalent	32-597
$26 \times 1\frac{3}{8} \times 1\frac{1}{8}$	$650 \times 28A$	28-590
$26 \times 1\frac{3}{8}$	$650 \times 35A$	35-590
$26 \times 1\frac{1}{2} \times 1\frac{1}{4}$	$650 \times 32B$	32-584
$26 \times 1.5*$	—	37-559
$26 \times 2.125*$	—	54-559
	$600 \times 28A$	28-541
$24 \times 1\frac{3}{8}$	—	32-540
$24 \times 1.75*$	—	44-507

*are mountain-bike sizes; nearly all adult-size mountain-bikes have 559mm diameter rims

(Below) A selection of cycle tyres showing the
extraordinary variety now manufactured.

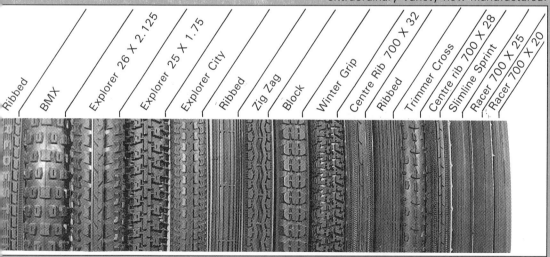

Ribbed · BMX · Explorer 26 X 2.125 · Explorer 25 X 1.75 · Explorer City · Ribbed · Zig Zag · Block · Winter Grip · Centre Rib 700 X 32 · Ribbed · Trimmer Cross · Centre rib 700 X 28 · Slimline Sprint · Racer 700 X 25 · Racer 700 X 20

Touring bicycles

While you can use practically any bike for leisure riding, a specialized style of touring bike has evolved over the years. The frame has moderate angles (basically 72 or 73° for average adult sizes) with clearances to accommodate comfortable 28 to 35mm-wide touring tyres, plus additional space for mudguards. It will also probably have brazed-on fittings for bag carriers and mudguards, for brake and gear cable guides, for bottle cages, for gear levers and for cantilever brakes. Handlebars are similar to racing ones, perhaps with a shallower drop and a shorter stem to give a more relaxed position.

Touring can involve all sorts of terrain, so touring bikes have a wide range of gears, including some very low ones for long or steep hills. A typical range covers a ratio of about 3 to 1 between the highest and the lowest, say 27 or 28 to 75 or 80 inches (2.2 to 6 or 6.4 metres development). Double or now more often triple front chainrings are standard, with five or six-speed freewheels; a personal favourite combination is 46-38-28 front chainrings used with a 16-18-20-22-25-28 freewheel.

(Opposite) A Dawes touring cycle. Touring cycles are designed for relaxing riding. Riders will be grateful for the full mudguard protection in wet weather. (Top left) A ladies' touring cycle. Note the difference in the frame. The top tube is here at a lower angle and divided. (Top right) Riding off the beaten track on a touring bike. (Right) A Dawes tandem. Tandems can allow riders of different abilities to cycle together.

Mountain-bikes

The mountain or all-terrain bike has the most distinctive profile of all. No-one could mistake the chunky tyres, solid frame, flat bars and beefed-up components. In many ways mountain bikes are like special-purpose touring ones; they have a wide gear range and are certainly robust. Triple chainwheels are virtually standard, 48-38-28 is common, usually combined with a six-speed freewheel running from 14 to 32 teeth. The stout wheels, with their 1.5 to 2.125 in (37–54 mm) wide tyres are designed to take a range of rough surfaces in their stride, while the bottom bracket is deliberately placed $1-1\frac{1}{2}$ in (25–35mm) higher than on other bicycles to clear rocks and ruts. Clearances between wheels and the frame are wide to avoid clogging with mud or other debris. Although not usually fitted as standard, mudguards and bag carriers are available. All have brazed-on cantilever brakes and handlebar controls for the indexed gears.

While many of the ideas incorporated into the mountain–bike are far from new, the fillip they gave to the industry in the second half of the 1980s proved just the impetus needed for manufacturers to produce in quantity the components that touring cyclists have requested for a long time. Not that mountain-bikes are only for leisure riding: many are used for everyday town trips (where they cope very well with ill-maintained street edges), while there are also specialised competition machines, often still evolving as riders continually feed in their own personal ideas.

(Opposite) A Carrera mountain-bike. The spectacular success of the mountain-bike derives not only from its off-the-road capabilities. It also copes very well with town and city problems. (Top left) Hill descents can be exciting. (Bottom left) In Central Africa. (Above) In the mountains.

Racing bicycles

The top-class racing bike is the thoroughbred of bicycles. Speed, responsiveness to a call for sudden acceleration and lightness are its hallmarks. Pared of unnecessary components, a fully-equipped road bike may weigh around 19–20 lbs (8.5–9 kg) and a track bike even less. Frame angles are around 74 or 75° and clearances between wheels and the frame close, with a short wheelbase – about 38–39 in (97–99 cm). In the chase for lightness the frame may be built using very thin gauges of very strong alloy steel tube (such as Reynolds 753 or 653), or more exotic materials such as aluminium alloys or carbon-fibre composites. Tyres are either very light wired-ons or tubulars. Wheels may be lightened by using fewer spokes – as low as 24 per wheel for good surfaces, with 28 and 32 quite common.

Gear ratios are much higher and more closely spaced than touring ones, though they can obviously be varied to match the race terrain. Double front chainrings are almost always used (although the outstanding French woman champion Jeannie Longo used a triple with spectacular success), usually in combination with a 7-speed freewheel. Typical chainwheel/sprocket combinations are 53-39 or 52-42 × 12-13-14-15-16-17-18. (A close ratio freewheel like this is often called a 'straight-through block' in Britain and much more picturesquely a 'corn-cob cluster' in the USA.) In a hilly race the largest three or four sprockets may be more widely spaced, typically to 12-13-14-15-17-19-22. Unlike the cantilever brakes fitted to touring and mountain bikes, those on racing bikes are nearly always of the scissor-action sidepull type.

One very specialized type of racing bicycle for use on a banked track is even simpler. Track bikes have even steeper frame angles and tight clearances, no brakes and no freewheel. The transmission is – just as on Starley's Rover Safety back in 1885 – a single chainring and a single fixed sprocket. Different gears are chosen (by changing the chainring or sprocket) according to the nature of the race and the ability of the rider. Typical combinations are 50 or 51 × 15. For special events on very smooth surfaces, tyres may be as light as 100 g.

Even more specialized bicycles have recently been developed for solo speed riding – time-trials on the road, pursuit racing and record-breaking on the track. These designs make use of the latest findings on reducing wind resistance, with components such as spokeless disc wheels.

Finally, note that most manufacturers include in their ranges bikes which are modelled on true road-racing machines but have lower specification components. They have basically the frame geometry of a racing bike, although the tubing quality may well not be top-notch, probably some sort of compromise gearing (42/52 × 14 to 24 is common) and heavier wheels. They may also have mudguards or fittings for them, and larger wheel clearances than a true racing bike. These really fit more into the category of sports/training bicycles.

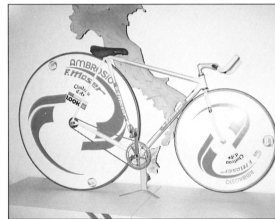

(Right) A Carrera Corsa racer model, a typical mass produced bike based on a true road racing machine. (Above) The special bike on which Moser set the world hour record. (Top) Colin Sturgess on a pursuit bike.

Choosing a bike

There are three fundamental questions you have to ask yourself before choosing a bicycle: what you want to use it for, what size you need to fit your own personal dimensions, and how much you are prepared to pay.

Purpose

You may have a particular use that makes it obvious what sort of bike would suit you best: you might want to ride off-road, say, in which case a mountain-bike is the choice, or to try racing. But if you're not so sure, choice might not be so easy. It is possible to change most components on a bicycle, so if you are interested mainly in touring, say, and buy a touring bike it would be quite possible to fit lighter wheels for faster riding or even to strip it down for dabbling in club time-trialling. Generally speaking, a touring bike is the most suitable for most general riding, such as travel to work, and some gentle off-road riding. Many urban riders are using mountain–bikes, partly through fashion, partly because they are robust. It would be worth fitting mudguards(US:fenders) in British and western European conditions. It is also not too difficult to adapt one of the racing-style sports machines for touring or regular riding. Once again you would need to fit mudguards and almost certainly lower gears. Don't forget the possible solution of two bicycles. It may well be cheaper and easier to have two specialized ones for the different things you want to do than to spend time and money in trying to adapt to an all-purpose compromise.

Size

This is utterly fundamental. Unless the frame size is correct for you, you will never find cycling as enjoyable as it should be. Frame size is measured in Britain and the USA as the distance from the centre of the bottom-bracket axle to the top of the seat lug, which is the top of the frame into which the saddle pillar fits. (In continental Europe the height is measured to the centre line of the frame top tube, which gives a value about 15mm less.) A useful rule of thumb is that this frame size should be about two-thirds (0.67 or 67%) of your full inside leg measurement, from

Not all bike commuting is as attractive as this, but bike commuting in today's congested cities can certainly be time and cost effective.

crutch to ground in bare feet. This allows for a reasonable amount of saddle pillar adjustment and most importantly, ensures that you can stand comfortably astride the bicycle with both feet on the ground. Because of their higher bottom bracket design, mountain-bikes call for a frame size about $1\frac{1}{2}$–2 in (35–50 mm) smaller than you would choose for a conventional bike.

Normally the other dimensions of the frame will be in proportion, at least in sizes down to

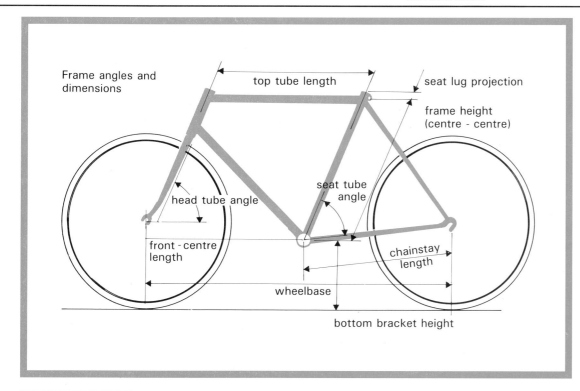

Frame angles and dimensions

top tube length

seat lug projection

frame height (centre - centre)

head tube angle

seat tube angle

front-centre length

chainstay length

wheelbase

bottom bracket height

The main measurements of a bicycle frame. British frame sizes are measured to the top of the seat lug: other countries measure centre-to-centre. Mountain bike frames have high bottom brackets, and shallower frame angles.

about 21 in (53 cm). Below this, small riders and in particular women, may have difficulty in finding an off-the-peg frame in which the top tube length (normally about the same as or slightly shorter than the frame size) is short enough. Generally, seat angles are steeper and head angles shallower on small frames (and the reverse on large ones) which helps, but there comes a point a which it is impossible, with normal (700C) diameter wheels, to make the top tube short enough without introducing unacceptable overlap between the feet and the front wheel. There are now a few firms making small frames to take either a small front wheel or small front and rear wheels (26 in/650 or, more usually, 24 in/600). If you can afford to go to a custom builder (below) you are more likely to get a small frame that really fits you.

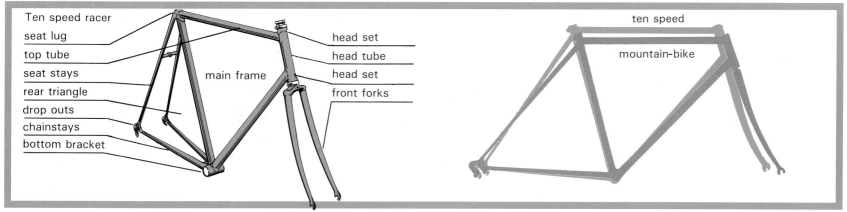

Ten speed racer

seat lug

top tube

seat stays

rear triangle

drop outs

chainstays

bottom bracket

main frame

head set

head tube

head set

front forks

ten speed

mountain-bike

Buying a bike

You should always buy a bike from a bike shop. That may seem obvious, but there are other outlets such as multiple stores and general mail order firms, who are unlikely to have the knowledge to give you advice nor to be able to offer after-sales service.

The least expensive way to buy a bicycle is to select a standad model from one of the well-known ranges, which nowadays offer good-quality models of all types, with very good-class components on the top-of-the-range machines. It can be cheaper to have alterations made to a standard model by the dealer (different gear ratios fitted, a change of saddle etc) than to have a custom-built bicycle. Manufacturers buy parts in bulk and can offer complete bicycles for a fraction of the retail cost of the frame and components. This is particularly true of mountain bikes.

Nevertheless there is particularly in Britain and France a tradition of small artisan builders who make custom-built frames or bicycles at an affordable price. (Many enthusiasts buy a frame and components and build up their own personalized machines, which can be quite fascinating and very satisfying if you know what you're doing.) Such a builder will short-cut your worries about sizing by making personal measurements, or seating you on an adjustable mock-up, and building the frame accordingly. Most moderate-sized towns have such a builder or an agent for one, and they are often listed in the cycling press. A good dealer will discuss

It pays to buy your cycle from a bike shop.

with you what you want the bicycle for and advise on the best course to follow.

Costs change with time of course, but the considerable amount of hand work in bicycle manufacture means that prices follow labour costs pretty closely. A decent-quality bicycle from a large manufacturer costs between one and a half and two times the average weekly wage, and a custom-built one from two to two

and a half upwards. By the time you're into carbon fibre and exotic disc wheels you can be well up ino the thousands of pounds or dollars (but don't forget fitness for purpose: the very expensive machine may not be the best for what you want to do). In general, mountain bikes are some twenty per cent dearer, specification for specification, than conventional semi-racing or touring ones.

Artisan builders flourish in Britain and France.
(Left) A racing trike. (Top) A tandem trike. These
unusual machines are only built in small
numbers. (Above) A carbon fibre racing bike. All
three machines are artisan designed and built.

Comfort and efficiency

There are three principal factors which determine how comfortable you will be on a bicycle, and how efficient your effort. They are: *your riding position on the machine*, which varies with the type of riding; *one or two critical components* such as saddles; and *clothing*.

Setting up a bike

The frame size of the bicycle is the basic key to setting up a comfortable and efficient riding position. What you have to do next is to make use of the various adjustments to get it just right. If you're buying a custom-built bike these points will have been taken into account in designing it, and in any case a good bike shop should make sure that your position is right before you leave the shop.

Saddle height is the first to be set. This is adjusted by undoing the bolt on the frame which clamps the seat pillar, moving the pillar up or down as needed, and then retightening the bolt, firmly but not excessively. The aim is to achieve a position where the leg is close to full extension at its lowest point but not stretched.

It is extremely important that you choose a bike with the correct frame size. This should be taken care of if you buy a bike from a reputable bike shop. There are several ways to set the saddle height, which are explained in the text.

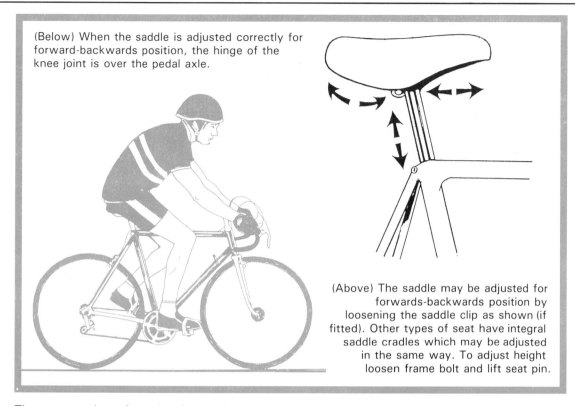

(Below) When the saddle is adjusted correctly for forward-backwards position, the hinge of the knee joint is over the pedal axle.

(Above) The saddle may be adjusted for forwards-backwards position by loosening the saddle clip as shown (if fitted). Other types of seat have integral saddle cradles which may be adjusted in the same way. To adjust height loosen frame bolt and lift seat pin.

If you are of average height, to determine correct frame size, straddle bike in bare feet. Between top frame tube and crotch there should be about an inch of clearance.

There are various formulae for setting saddle height based on ergometer studies. These give a roughly similar result: that the distance from the centre of the pedal axle to the top of the saddle, measured along the seat tube when the crank is near its lowest but aligned with the seat tube, should be nine percent greater than the inside leg measurement (measured as for frame sizing). This gives a height that is fine for short-distance racing but is a bit high for longer races and for touring, where a figure of six or seven per cent is nearer. The saddle top shold be hori-zontal throughout any of these adjustments, and it should obviously point straight ahead.

The next to be set is the forward/backward position of the saddle. Provided your frame is the right size, so that its seat angle is appropriate you are unlikely to have to move it far. The adjustment is made by loosening the bolt or bolts on the seat pillar which grip the longitudi-nal frame wires of the saddle and sliding it forwards or backwards, again retightening firmly once the move has been made. The check of the most effective position is that the hinge of the forward knee joint should be directly over the centre of the pedal axle when you are sitting properly on the saddle and the cranks are hori-zontal. For gentle riding and touring you may find it more comfortable to sit up to $\frac{3}{4}$ in (20 mm) further back. Persist with the saddle in this position for a while unless it is utterly uncomfor-table, and make any further adjustments in small steps. Resist any temptation to adjust the saddle very far from the horizontal.

The final stage concerns handlebar position. This varies a great deal according to the type of

(Right) How to determine the correct stem length.

riding. Dropped bars allow you a choice of position: holding the bottom part for effort or riding into a headwind, where the more streamlined shape exposes a smaller frontal area to the wind, or holding the brake levers or the tops of the bars for more relaxed riding. Indeed, you hardly use the bottom part for touring. The length of the handlebar stem also affects your position. Since upper body length in relation to leg length varies quite widely (and tends to be different in women and men) it is possible to give universal rules. The best starting point is to set the top of the handlebar about level with the saddle (possibly slightly lower if you are very tall). This should then give you a relaxed position when you have your hands on the top of the bars with your upper body at about 45° to the horizontal, which is fine for general riding and touring. Racing also involves spending quite a bit of the the time in this position but flat-out effort holding the drops will probably call for a rather rather longer handlebar stem. This component is a relatively easy one to replace if necessary. If you want to race you will have in any case to join a club (see page 154) and the club coach or other experienced members will undoubtedly be able to advise you in detail.

A bicycle set up in this way should allow you to develop a fluid pedalling style so that you transmit power to the pedals smoothly without undue upper body movement. Cultivate riding with your elbows slightly bent: this helps to protect your neck and shoulders from road shocks

Handlebar adjustment. (1). Height. Loosen stem bolt and tap down with hammer and wood block. Twist stem to raise or lower. (2). The stem length is fixed and cannot be adjusted. (3) Tilt. Loosen bolts at front of stem. Turn handlebars.

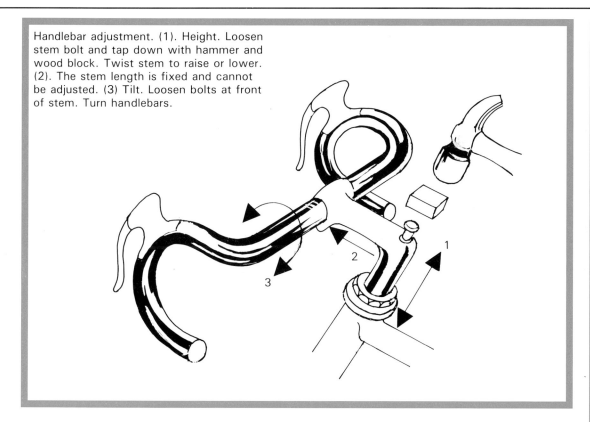

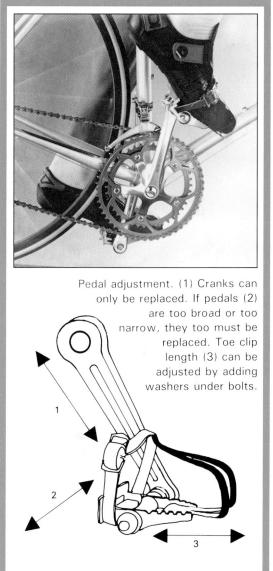

Pedal adjustment. (1) Cranks can only be replaced. If pedals (2) are too broad or too narrow, they too must be replaced. Toe clip length (3) can be adjusted by adding washers under bolts.

far more effectively than excessive handlebar padding. Develop as well the use of gear ratios which let you *pedal* rather than push. At normal cruising road speeds your pedalling rhythm should be somewhere in the 70 to 90 rpm range.

The fact that at the optimum saddle position defined earlier the pedal-to-saddle distance is actually *greater* than the inside leg length underlines the part that the foot and ankle play in pedalling. For correct pedalling, the ball of the foot – the large joint at the base of the big toe –

has to be over the pedal axle. This soon becomes quite natural and is helped by positive devices which hold the foot in the right place such as toe-clips and straps, shoeplates (US: cleats) which slot over the plates of conventional pedals, or ski-binding-type pedals of the type pioneered by Look, in which a fitting on the sole of the shoe snaps into a recess on the pedal. Beginners should start with toeclips and straps with smooth-soled shoes until the pick-up action on starting becomes automatic.

Saddles

The function of a saddle is to support your weight via the ischial bones at the base of the pelvic girdle while at the same time allowing your legs free movement. This means that a saddle *must* be wide enough at the back for the more-or-less flat part to engage both the ischial bosses. The separation of these bones varies a lot between individuals (and they are generally more widely spaced in women than in men), so that choice of saddle can be highly personal. You will almost certainly find that some other people will find your comfortable saddle quite uncomfortable, and vice versa. Don't therefore, accept even well-meant advice as gospel for you. Most riders find a fairly firm but not hard saddle comfortable, one that gives definite support and does not tend to spread under load (which can lead to chafing of the inside of the thighs). Many women find shorter saddles more comfortable.

The traditional saddle, which many riders still favour, was made from leather and needed a 'breaking in' period to make it comfortable. Modern nylon saddles can be made directly to the right resilience and have a variety of padded, non-slip and decorative coverings. Racing cyclists sit relatively lightly on the saddle.

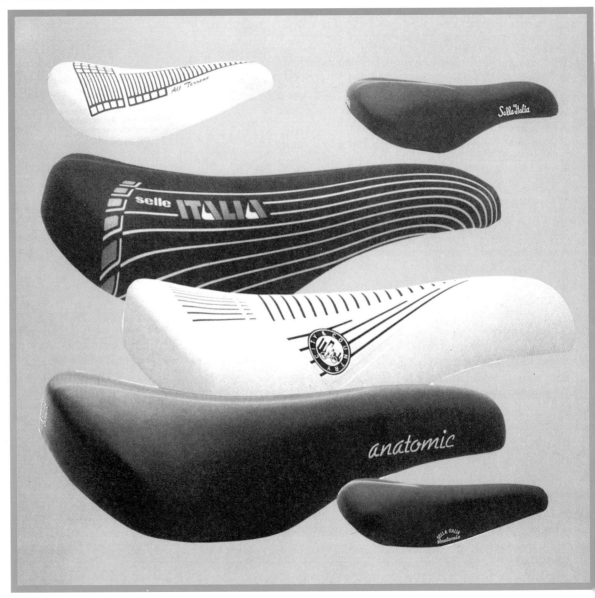

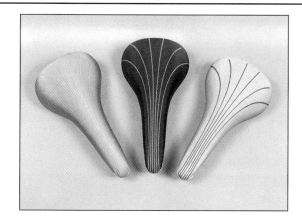

Shorts and trousers

The other great aids to seat comfort are properly-designed cycling shorts and trousers. Most conventional garments and underwear have seams which come at just the wrong place: transverse seams are the worst. Shorts and trousers meant for cycling are cut to avoid such seams and have a smooth inner lining. The traditional lining is chamois leather but there are now also cotton and polyester substitutes which are much less temperamental in washing. These linings are available in padded or unpadded form; which you pick is a matter of choice, since some riders find the bulkiness of the padding uncomfortable. Nowadays shorts are usually in a nylon-elastomer mix ('skin-shorts') and close-fitting cycling trousers either in similar material or in nylon/cotton or acrylic mixes. If you do not fancy the figure-hugging skin-shorts, shorts with suitable linings are available in other materials, or separate skin-short-style inner shorts are on the market. Shorts etc with these linings are intended to be worn next to the skin – wearing seamed underwear inside them rather defeats the object – and naturally require to be washed frequently.

(Top and left) Modern saddles are only two thirds the weight of older leather saddles. Today's racing saddles may weigh as little as 350 grams.

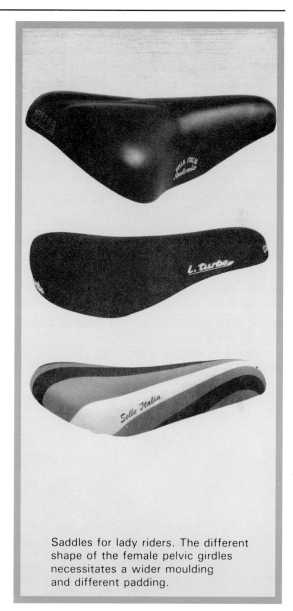

Saddles for lady riders. The different shape of the female pelvic girdles necessitates a wider moulding and different padding.

Other clothing for cycling

Cycling is an athletic pursuit. This means that the exercise makes you warm. However, a cyclist moves through the air much faster than a runner and so suffers from speed-induced wind-chill effects. The degree to which people sweat under effort varies enormously between individuals, but in effect all clothing worn for cycling has to be windproof enough to keep you warm on the downhill swoops (depending of course on the weather and air temperature) while at the same time being light and porous enough to let you cool by sweating on the uphills. Most riders find that this is most easily met by wearing the appropriate number of layers of fairly thin garments. Most purpose-made cycling tops are based roughly on road-racing cyclists' jerseys and are made usually of acrylic or fleecy-backed polyester. More importantly, though, purpose-made tops are cut long enough at the back to allow for the forward-leaning riding position and to avoid exposing the readily-chilled lower back.

(Right) Racing shoes with nylon soles (to keep their shape) and with leather insoles.

(Left) Mountain bikes shoes for the roughest conditions. Tough, warm and waterproof, with a special ankle collar to protect the tendons.

(Below) Overshoes have become an accepted wear in cold and wet weather. Lycra overshoes are popular with tourists and commuters.

(Left) Racing jerseys are also popular off-the-track. In fact cycle-style clothing is now very fashionable.

(Above) Gloves can be extremely useful in cold weather. Nylon mittens can be even warmer.

(Below) Typical winter clothing. Most purpose-made cycling tops are made from acrylic or fleecy-backed polyester.

Cold and wet weather

The wind-chill effect gives cyclists particular problems in cold or wet weather. The effects of wind-chill are much worse when the body or clothing are wet and it's possible to become very chilled even on quite a warm day by plunging downhill in wet clothing. The wind-chill also means that body extremities which are not warmed by effort also cool rapidly.

Once more personal metabolism enters into it. Riders who sweat readily find the best course in cold weather is to add more but still porous layers. These allow sweat to escape, while the overlapping layers offer some windproofing. Riders who sweat less may find windproof jackets or tops satisfactory over rather fewer layers. Polypropylene undervests, which wick moisture away from the skin, can help in very cold weather. Removing the sweat does, however, inhibit the body's natural cooling mechanism so that you have to keep an eye on possible overheating. Quite a lot of heat is dissipated from the head – it's even been described as the radiator of the body engine – so that wearing, or not wearing, a hat can help adjust heat loss.

Non-porous gloves can make hands clammy and most riders find combinations of wool with slightly porous ski gloves or nylon-fleece mitts satisfactory. Cold feet can be alleviated by wearing an extra pair of socks and a size larger shoe or by putting windproof overshoes over feet and ankles. Acrylic or polypropylene tights, worn between shorts and trousers, can help to keep legs warm. The age-old remedy of walking up a hill instead of riding can restore cold feet.

Wet weather, too, poses problems for cyclists. Indeed, rain along with hills and traffic, is often quoted as one of the commonest factors discouraging would-be cyclists. Being wet is not of itself uncomfortable (nobody complains about a warm bath!) but the increased potential for chilling certainly can be. Claims for miracle fabrics notwithstanding, anything which is going to keep rain out is going to keep perspiration in or at least retard its escape. Because the body is no longer subject to wind-chill once it's wrapped in an impervious outer it soon heats up. Hence, despite all its disadvantages in wind and traffic (it's virtually unusable in city riding) the old-fashioned voluminous all-covering cape, which

(Above and right) The traditional cape is perhaps the best wet-weather compromise.

allows some air circulation round the body, is as good a compromise as any for all but the shortest journeys. But it is not only from above that the wet-weather cyclist is assaulted; road spray also comes from underneath onto legs and feet. Properly fitted mudguards with an effective front flap are essential. Overshoes can once more help protect feet but the really effective waterproof trouser set for cyclists has yet to be designed. Probably the best principle for at least short-term wetness is to try to concentrate on keeping warm and then be sure to change into dry clothing at the earliest opportunity.

Safe cycling

Most countries regard the bicycle as part of the road traffic, logically with rights and obligations part-way between those of the pedestrian and the car driver. Details of the law as it applies to cyclists vary from country to country (and often from state to state in the USA, where some individual states have quite capricious restrictions or requirements). Cyclists, like the rest of the traffic, are everywhere required to obey traffic signs and signals. Don't assume that, because you are on a bicycle, red lights, stop signs and 'no entry' injunctions don't apply to you. They do. Take particular care when joining major roads and observe 'give way' (US: yield) signs. In most countries (but not in general in Britain) cyclists are required to use cycle paths beside the road if they exist.

British law requires your bicycle to have efficient brakes, with independent front and rear braking systems, if it is to be used on the road. Most other countries have a similar requirement, although in some northern European countries a single rear pedal-operated hub brake is acceptable. Bicycles are required to carry front and rear lights complying with designated standards if used at night, while further regulations govern the placing and type of reflectors. As a safeguard to users, lamps and reflectors that do not comply

Riding at dusk or at night it is important that you can see and be seen. Dark or drab clothing makes you much less visible. Make sure your lights and reflectors are kept clean and not obscured.

with the standards may not be sold as cycle equipment.

More information is readily available in *The Highway Code* in Britain, the *Code de la route* in France and comparable publications in other countries. These contain specific advice for cyclists as well as for other road users.

Quite a deal of attention is focused by outside bodies and even by some cycling ones on protective wear, particularly helmets and 'conspicuity aids'. Bicycle helmets are intended to offer some protection in the case of a fall from the bicycle; neither manufacturers nor testers claim efficacy in more violent impacts from motor vehicles. Opinions are divided as to their efficacy in protection from closed-head injury – that is, injury resulting from rapid deceleration – and as to their other effects on vision, hearing and ventilation. (Opinions are also divided as to their desirability in directing attention to the victim rather than the cause of accidents.) The view of major cycling organizations is that using one must remain the choice of the individual. The most rigorous testing of helmets has been carried out by the Snell Institute in the United States and cyclists who choose to wear one are recommended to use one conforming to Snell requirements. In general, bright and light-coloured upper body clothing, which instinctively and immediately conveys the human shape to drivers, is quite as effective as fluorescent belts and so on. It is important that neither helmet nor 'conspicuity aid' should be looked on as some sort of magic talisman, conferring immunity on the wearer. Much more of your safety lies in your own hands.

(Above) A rear reflector and rear light. Unless lamps and reflectors comply with current safety regulations they may not be sold as cycle equipment.

(Left) Tyres with reflective bands can be brilliantly picked up by car headlights. This can reduce the risk of being hit side-on.

(Top) An aerodynamic racing helmet popular with time-triallists and triathletes. Usually made with polycarbonate shell. (Above) The traditional racing helmet.

Riding techniques

Your own riding technique is your biggest contribution to safe cycling. You have to learn to be fully in control of the bicycle at all times. The first technique to be learnt and practised is riding in straight line, or smooth curve, without wobbling. This means learning to relax: a properly set-up bike with everything in alignment should virtually steer itself. Your weight distribution, as much as turning the handlebars, then determines the line you will follow. For example, if you freewheel, lift the left-hand pedal and put most of your weight on the lower, right, one, the bicycle will automatically lean slightly to the left and turn left. The opposite action turns you right, and as you become more adept and more at home you will gradually come to feel that no more than the lightest correction on the handlebars is necessary in straight-line riding.

A bicycle is less stable when it is cornering than when it is going straight ahead. When cornering there are sideways forces acting on it which are countered by the friction of the tyres on the road; the faster you corner the more acutely you will need to lean and the greater these forces will be – and the more dependent you will be on the grip of the tyres. This means that you must learn to be circumspect if the surface is doubtful – smooth and wet, or with loose gravel or fallen leaves. Watch out, too, for road studs, metal inspection covers, low kerbs across some side-road entrances, drains and so on. If the road surface is deteriorating, potholes (US: road craters, chuckholes) tend to develop first and worst on corners, where the tyres of cars

A racing cyclist in a steep turn, showing the sideways force acting on bike and rider. These are countered by the friction of the tyres on the road. Avoid hard cornering if you are not sure of the surface.

and other vehicles are tending to scrub the surface away.

A bicycle is also less stable when it is braking, so braking should be carried out as far as possible before you get to the corner or junction. Learn to use the brakes gently and progressively, not snatching them on. The front brake is the one that does the stopping: as you decelerate, more of your weight acts on the front wheel, making the front brake the more effective. The rear brake is used to supplement the front brake but is most effective when you are not decelerating, when it is used to hold speed steady, on a long downhill for example. You also have a third brake which can be quite effective, again on long downhills: an air brake. By sitting upright you can make use of the wind resistance to limit your speed. This works particularly well on long mountain passes which usually have moderate gradients and where using the hand brakes for perhaps ten miles (16km) can be quite tedious.

Brakes can be noticeably less effective, at least to begin with, in the wet. Modern brake block compounds improve performance as well as the use of light aluminium alloy rims which heat up rapidly and clear the film of moisture between the brake pad and the rim. It helps if you can anticipate the need for braking and apply the brakes early to dry out the braking surface of the rim.

Cultivate the proper use of the gears. The purpose of variable gears is to enable you to continue to pedal at a comfortable rate when gradient or wind slow or quicken your road

In an emergency use both brakes and brace your arms to keep your weight well back.

speed. Although the base pedalling rhythm is in the 70–90 range, there is a natural tendency to pedal slower at the bottom end of the road speed range and faster at the top. This means that in practice the 27 to 75 in (2.2 to 6 metre development) gear range suggested for a touring or mountain bike covers road speeds from something like walking pace, say 4 mph (6 kph) to perhaps 25 mph (40 kph). Change down as you approach a junction or sharp corner so that you can pull away comfortably from a slow speed or stop. Change down in good time on hills: you need to be pedalling at something like a minimum of 50 rpm to get a reasonable change. There's a knack to just easing the actual pressure on the pedals as you change gear, while still keeping your feet turning.

Climbing out of the saddle. The rider holds the brake hoods and puts his body weight rhythmically alternately onto left and right pedals, keeping the bike moving in a straight line.

Riding in traffic

Inevitably you will have to share the road with other traffic and a few simple rules and techniques can make it much easier and safer. Basically you must be aware of what is going on around you and then behave predictably in such a way that it is obvious to drivers and, come to that, other cyclists what you are doing.

● As far as possible ride briskly and decisively as part of the traffic stream. Don't cringe in the nearside gutter but make your presence and your intentions obvious by your placing on the road. Be predictable – but expect other road users to do the unexpected.

● Use a fairly upright riding position so that you can sit up and see what other traffic is doing. You might find a rear-view mirror helpful but don't forget that such fitments offer only a limited field of view. You will find with experience that you can often *hear* the line that vehicles coming from behind are taking. Ears are valuable: don't muffle them.

● Signal your intentions clearly and in good time *after* checking behind that your proposed move is possible and safe. It does help if you can catch the eye of whoever you're signalling to.

● Stay in your traffic lane unless you're preparing for a turn.

Great Britain is not yet well endowed with special lanes for cyclists, which are common in Holland.

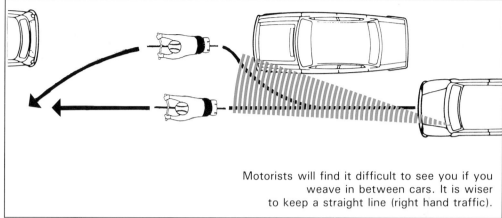

Motorists will find it difficult to see you if you weave in between cars. It is wiser to keep a straight line (right hand traffic).

● Take care when moving up between lines of stationary or slow-moving traffic. Watch for closing gaps that it would be unsafe to go into.
● Where possible, join major roads or leave them at junctions controlled by traffic lights. These allow you to move off as part of the traffic stream.
● At junctions make sure that you are in the correct traffic lane. If you are going straight ahead, don't obstruct a nearside lane from which traffic may be allowed to filter left, nor an offside one which may have a separate traffic light sequence. Don't place yourself on the left or right of waiting vehicles which have signalled that they are going to turn in these directions.
● Watch out for debris and poor road surfaces near the road edge. You must learn to ease yourself over rough patches rather than change your line.
● Concentrate your attention on what you are doing. Try to put other thoughts out of your mind for the time being.

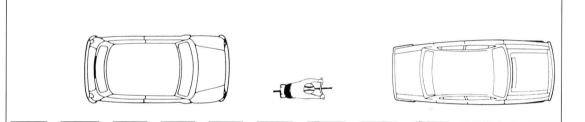

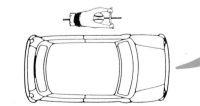

(Above) It is safer to ride in the flow of the traffic if riding as fast as the cars. (Below) Beware of cars cutting across you to turn left. Lights and reflectors help to protect you at night. (Left hand traffic).

Leisure cycling

The term 'leisure cycling' is used here rather than 'cycle touring' to emphasise the wide range of cycling just for pleasure. You don't have to embark on a 'tour' of a week or more: you could just be out for the afternoon or a couple of hours – the cycling analogue of a Sunday family walk. With the proliferation of the mountain bike, the analogue can be even closer.

Cycling is indeed really only geared-up walking – the bicycle extends the scope of your stroll, while still giving you the chance to look around you, hear the sounds of the countryside, even (since you are not insulated from the outside world by metal and glass) to smell its scents. And, unlike a car, a bicycle can stop pretty well anywhere. A comfortable five-mile (8 km) walk might be transformed into a 15-mile (25 km) cycle ride.

But cycling is a very practical means of transport, so that same bicycle is capable of carrying you much further. Even a very gentle 25 miles (40 km) per day can take you 175 miles (280 km) in a week; a still relatively leisurely 40 miles (65 km) could take you 560 miles (900 km) in a two-week trip.

All leisure cycling, though, is much more pleasurable if you choose quiet roads (and tracks), if you can carry easily what you need and ride within your capabilities.

The lure of the open road. A British cycling group taking part in a randonnée of the Montagne de Reims in France's Champagne Country.

Choosing a route

There are of course now many 'ready-made' cycle routes. Many local authorities, area tourist boards and others have researched routes for cyclists, waymarked them on the ground and produced explanatory leaflets. Examples include the Lancashire, Cheshire and Wiltshire cycleways – signed routes using minor roads and devised to take in places of interest as well as offering pleasant cycling. But half the fun of any sort of travel is in the anticipation and so, even if you include parts of waymarked routes on your trips, it's worth learning how to pick out a route for yourself.

This means using a suitable map. Britain is covered by a fine series of detailed maps at a scale of 1:50 000, the Ordnance Survey's Landranger series. At this scale, a mile is represented by about $1\frac{1}{4}$ in on the map, or 1 km by 2 cm. The scale is detailed enough to show virtually every road and track, together with details of villages, towns, churches, individual farms, woodland, streams, lakes and rivers, and other landmarks. 'Tourist information', such as places of interest, good viewpoints, and campsites are also marked, while the maps also show what every cyclist needs to know – how hilly the route may be.

Roads are shown in five colours, according to their status. Motorways, not open to cyclists, are marked in blue. Main A-roads are shown in red, with the major trunk roads marked '(T)'. The 'A'-grading covers a very wide range of road, from the three-lane dual carriageway which is a motorway in all but name to quite rural roads in

the more remote parts of the country. In general, in lowland Britain, avoid using A-roads as far as possible, and certainly avoid using long stretches of them. Roads in the next category, B-roads, are marked in brown. These, too, can vary from quite busy highways in or near towns, or where they offer a link between two A-roads, to pleasant quiet roads, once more usually in more remote or rural areas. It is the next category, the unclassified roads, coloured yellow, which are the most pleasant to cycle on. These are tarred hard-surfaced roads and are marked in two different widths on the map, according to whether they are wider or narrower than 4 metres. Road width doesn't matter much to a cyclist but the narrower ones are usually likely to carry less traffic. Another feature shown is whether or not a road is fenced (which includes hedges and walls); an unfenced road, particularly in rolling country, can suggest that it will offer more open views – but less shelter. The final category of road is uncoloured and includes minor roads of indifferent surface, minor streets in towns and unsurfaced tracks.

Hills and valleys are shown in three ways. Heights above sea level in metres ('spot heights') are shown at varying intervals. It's obviously uphill from a lower one to a higher, and you will soon develop the ability to judge how much effort a, say, 50-metre climb calls for. One of the simplest ways is to find from the map the climb involved in some local hills you know well and then evaluate unknown ones by comparison. (One traveling companion used even to

evaluate Alpine passes as so many Holme Mosses and Troughs of Bowland.) The second system of showing relief is the contour line. These are imaginary lines, marked in brown on the map, which link points of the same height. Although the map is metric, they are plotted at 50 ft (15.24 metre) intervals. The more closely grouped the contour lines, the steeper the slope. Finally, steep road gradients are shown by arrow or chevron marks: one chevron indicates slopes between 1 in 7 and 1 in 5 (14–20 per cent), while two mark a gradient steeper than 1 in 5 (over 20 per cent). These are quite steep hills. Disconcertingly for the cyclist (who wants to be warned of roads which go *up*) the arrows or chevrons point *downhill*.

Armed with this information it is now quite easy to work out on the map a simple route which follows minor roads, preferably only crossing A-roads and not following them, and which is not too hilly. Following the route on the road may be a halting progress at first as you stop to verify your position at junctions but you will soon get the feel for how far a given length on the map feels on the road. You may find a mileage recorder ('cyclometer') or one of the new 'cycle computers' a help in showing how far you have travelled between such checks, or how far you have to travel to the next turn.

(Opposite, right) A mountain biker in a beechwood at Penn, Buckinghamshire in the Chilterns. Cyclists in Britain have legal right of way on bridle paths. (Opposite, left) A minor road near Chedworth in the Cotswolds.

The only drawback with these OS maps is that they are a little awkward to refold so that they can be consulted on the bike, calling for a doubling-back of the folded form in which they're supplied if you want to have one or two panels exposed. There are several ways of carrying maps on a bicycle. Map carriers are available which clip to the handlebars and hold the opened and folded map. Most handlebar bags (below) have a transparent pocket on top to hold a map or route instructions. We have also found the apparently crude expedient of using an elastic strap to hold the map in place on top of a front carrier to be remarkably effective and convenient. Alternatively, if you have a large enough pocket (such as the one on a cycling top) you can carry the map in that, taking it out as necessary.

The same principles apply to maps of other countries, although obviously the details differ. The various European countries have their own official series of maps, directly comparable to the British Ordnance Survey ones and at similar scales. Some, such as France and Switzerland, also produce maps at the near-ideal scale for the cyclist of 1:100 000 (1 cm on the map representing 1 km on the ground, or just over $\frac{1}{2}$ inch to the mile). Quite a few European countries are also well covered by maps produced by commercial companies; for example, the French Michelin maps with their distinctive yellow covers embrace not only France, but Switzerland, the Netherlands, Belgium and Luxembourg, together with parts of western Germany,

at a scale of 1:200 000. Road classifications in most European countries are comparable: major roads are often designated 'National' and are similar to British A-roads, with varying designations for minor ones. They are easily distinguished by colour: red is almost universal for main routes and yellow or uncoloured for minor roads. All of course give distances in kilometres and heights in metres. Methods of indicating relief and hilliness of roads vary.

In the broader spaces of north America things are a little different. The United States Geological Survey and the Canadian Government Department of Energy, Mines and Resources both produce detailed maps comparable to the European ones. However, the much greater distances to be covered mean that it is not practicable for cyclists to equip themselves with, say, all the 1:50 000 sheets needed for a trip. Equally, in any case, the much less dense road network, away from centres of population, means that a cyclist needs in practice less information for route following. Many states produce moderate-scale motoring maps which vary in usefulness with the terrain. The Rand-McNally commercially-produced series covers the whole of the United States, state by state. The various National Parks publish more detailed maps as do the motoring organisations.

One US cycling organization, Bikecentennial, produces detailed maps specifically for cyclists at a scale of 1:250 000, with information on the terrain, climate, history and facilities of the region printed on the reverse. These maps take

the form of panels and are in effect strip maps covering researched and recommended routes located on the east and west coasts, together with two trans-continental routes. They are essentially linear one-way journeys, rather than circular tours. (It's worth noting that prevailing winds often mean that a route is better followed in one direction than the other. Almost everybody who chooses a Pacific Coast route, for example, travels from north to south.) Each map panel shows details for about 4–6 miles on either side of the recommended route. Bikecentennial supplies these maps to members and also act as stockists for locally-produced maps and guides, often prepared by local bicycle organizations or cyclists, covering smaller areas in more detail.

Because of the scarcity of roads in any areas it is not possible to recommend routes which avoid all major roads (in the United States the Interstate and US Federal Highways). In any case these often carry quite light traffic by European standards, while most have wide marked shoulders on which cyclists can ride, while passing motor traffic follows the centre lanes. Their main drawback is often that in open country they can be tryingly straight for very long distances indeed, with little or no shelter and with settlements many miles apart. Nevertheless, there are often alternative smaller roads

(Opposite left) A Dutch landscape at Bergen-op-Zoom. (Opposite right) Connemara, County Galway, Ireland. Although this countryside can be quite wild, it offers fairly easy cycling.

– State or Provincial Highways, or the even more minor county and local roads. In the more remote areas, these smaller roads are often untarred (US: unpaved) and may have gravel or oil- or water-bound earth surfaces. The state of these varies with the season and the weather – but don't expect to hurry along them. Most north American maps differentiate between paved and unpaved roads. Note that Canada is officially metric, so distances are given in kilometres, both on the maps and on road signs, and heights in metres. Canada is also officially bilingual, so that even well away from the French-speaking south-east, major road signs can be in both English and French. United States maps and signs usually give distances in miles and heights in feet, although some National Park information is given in metric measures.

Off-road routes

With the rise of the mountain bike there has been widespread interest in off-road routes. The 1968 Countryside Act in the UK permitted cyclists to ride on bridleways (subject to a requirement to give way to walkers and horse-riders where necessary), while byways open to all traffic are also obviously available to cyclists.

The tough but rewarding route by Loch Avich to Loch Awe in Scotland. Scotland is a superb area for touring offering a great variety of landscape. (Opposite) An expedition using mountain bikes in Zaire.

These byways have the status of roads but the local authority is not required to maintain them as surfaced roads. A third category, the 'road used as public path' is gradually disappearing as such 'RUPP's are regarded as byways, bridleways or footpaths. The OS 1:50 000 sheets and the sister Pathfinder 1:25 000 maps give details of these public rights of way. (This information applies only to England and Wales; under Scottish law, right of way can depend on evidence of continuous usage. The CTC publication *Cycling off-road and the law* by Neil Horton gives more detail.) Certain long-distance trails incorporate long stretches of cyclable off-road route, notably the bridleway version of the South Downs Way and the section of the Ridgeway Path west of the River Thames. There are further plans afoot for other routes, including a bridleway version of the Pennine Way.

In addition to rights of way there are permissive routes such as canal towpaths (for which a permit has to be bought) and some forest trails in Forestry Commission woodland. A number of routes have been designated from the start as cycle routes, many of them offering traffic-free routes out of large towns, such as the Bath–Bristol path. Quite a few such routes follow the beds of former railway branches. In the Peak National Park two such routes are the Tissington and High Peak Trails which wind an almost level way into the hills.

It's not necessary to own a mountain bike to be able to follow many of these routes, which cyclists have been travelling for many years. The

mountain bike comes into its own on the rougher, stickier or looser-surfaced paths. This ability of the mountain bike rider to reach out into wilder places caused initially some conflict between mountain bike riders and walkers on some popular routes, and in 1989 the Sports Council and the Countryside Commission, in conjunction with cycling and mountain bike bodies, produced an advisory Mountain Bike Code intended to inform new mountain bike purchasers of the rights of way open to them and to give some practical advice on travel in wild places.

The attraction of these off-the-beaten track routes is that they can lead into remote and solitary places. But they should be treated with care.

Cycling out of season

One very simple method of finding quiet roads is to extend your cycling season beyond the summer months. Many popular areas are very quiet once the summer crowds have gone, while in Britain the spring and autumn are often drier. Certainly the different seasons offer quite new perspectives on the landscape and a whole new gamut of colour. In most parts, winter cycling can also be very enjoyable. There are periods at the beginning and end of winter where in the more mountainous parts of the country it can be colourful late autumn or early spring in the valleys while the tops of the hills are bright with winter snow. Cycling out of season can bring rewards of its own.

Days are, however, shorter and temperatures lower. This means that distances will have to be prepared for more extremes of weather. In mid-winter temperatures can begin to fall quite rapidly from perhaps 2.30 pm as the already low sun dips towards the horizon. You will find that gloves, a hat and an extra layer or two will be needed.

In fact, the seasons are rather later than the height of the sun in the sky would suggest. Generally the coldest weather is in early February, while mild autumn weather often extends until quite late in October. Autumn colours can continue until late November.

Descending to Banff, Alberta, Canada in the Rocky Mountains near Lake Minniewanka. The roads here often follow the river valleys so that gradients are less formidable than might be expected.

(Above) A member of the Freewheel 'World Wildlife' team pushes a mountain bike during a ten month, 1700 mile (2720km) journey from Alaska to Brazil. The bikes only suffered 3 broken spokes and 27 punctures. (Left) Crossing the Jotunheimen in Norway at 1400 metres. Ferries can help cyclists around Norway's fjords.

Carrying loads on a bike

If you are to travel for more than an afternoon you are almost certain to need to carry at least one or two items with you. Even for that afternoon trip it's worth having the minimal repair kit of a spare inner tube and tyre levers.

The golden rule is that the bicycle carries the baggage (although some mountain bike riders seem to prefer small rucksacks for off-road use). This means some sort of bag that can be fixed on and usually some sort of carrier (US: rack) to support it.

For light loads a small handlebar bag can be useful. This fits in front of the handlebars, preferably on a small carrier to keep it clear of the part of the bar you might want to hold and also clear of the front mudguard. These bags are usually about an 8 or 9-in (20–23 cm) cube, and are very handy for items you want to reach quickly. Most have little pockets for such things as gloves – plus the map pocket on top. Handlebar bags are not too easy to fit to mountain-bikes.

For rather larger loads you have the choice of a saddlebag, which fits transversely behind and below the saddle and above the rear carrier, or panniers, which fit either side of the carrier lower down. Both have advantages and disadvantages. Saddlebags carry the weight a little high but mostly within the wheelbase and clear of road dirt. They need to be packed carefully if they are not to sag lopsidedly and they have a limited capacity. They are the traditional British solution; they are best strapped to special bag loops on the saddle frame (which most current saddles lack). Panniers comprise two separate

A basic tool kit: a box spanner(US:wrench), tyre levers(US:tire irons) and 5 and 6 mm allen keys(US:hexagon wrenches).

A popular medium-sized saddle bag favoured by traditional tourists. The straps are leather and there will be an inner lining.

bags which are clipped or strapped on either side of the pannier carrier. They are available in a range of sizes, with the largest capable of carrying enormous loads. They have the advantage of carrying the load well down, which helps keep the bicycle's centre of gravity low as well, but can cause the bicycle to shake or 'shimmy', particularly if the carrier isn't rigid (although the ultimate cause of this odd vibration is rather more complex). The most rigid carriers are those which are triangulated in three dimensions.

Some mountain-bike users report problems if too large or too low-mounted panniers are used on rough or rutted ground.

It is also possible to fit panniers to the front wheel, in which case they are best mounted low down on an appropriate carrier. These are particularly useful as a counterbalance to rear loads, particularly when the total load is large, as when camping. Tests suggest that a weight distribution of two-thirds at the rear and one-third at the front gives the best stability.

Rear panniers
Cycle touring can be a great pleasure—if you are carrying all you need safely and comfortably. These rear panniers offer a 35 litre capacity. Note the reflective safety strips on the rear pockets. Panniers are usually made from waterproofed nylon.

Bar bag
Handlebar bags sometimes have transparent map holders which can be useful. Shoulder straps make them handy for off-bike use.

Front bags
These can be used on low riders or could also be used as small rear panniers. There are external zippered pockets.

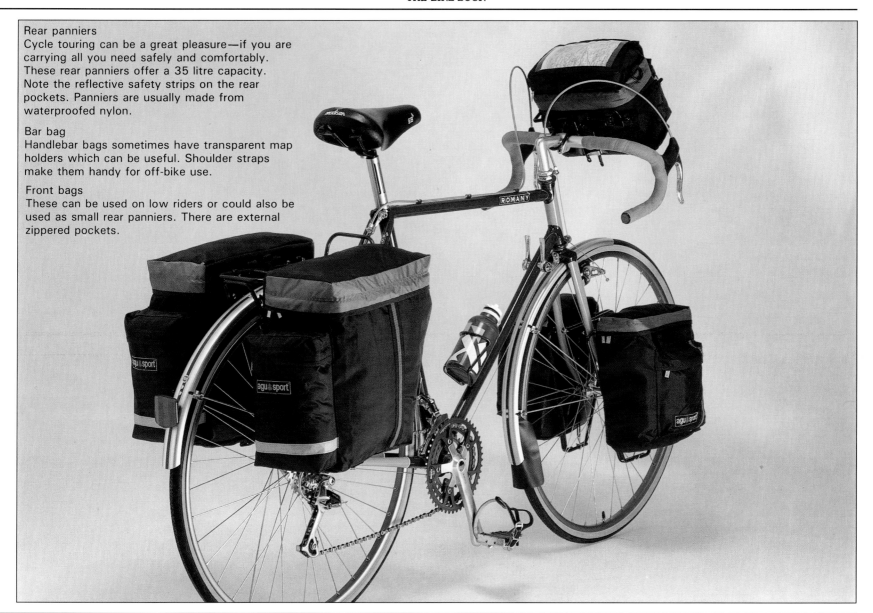

Taking it steady

(Below) On the historic Ridgeway, England.
(Right) Idyllic scene nr. Great Bedwyn, Wiltshire, England.

Leisure cycling is a long way from racing but even so you are using energy. You will find it a great deal more enjoyable if you ride within your capabilities – which will increase rapidly with experience. This means not trying to travel too fast or too far to begin with. The fact that the bicycle supports quite a lot of your body weight can lull you into feeling you can travel further than you easily can – whereas had you been walking your weary legs would have given a warning. It is best to begin with trips you are sure you can manage easily – perhaps as little as 5 miles (8 km) – and then work up. Trying to go too fast can make any road hard, so ride gently,

in a low enough gear that your legs are turning steadily at the 70 or so rpm suggested earlier. You will soon find that you have a natural easy cruising speed (and gear) at which you feel comfortable. This speed will possibly increase as you become more practised.

These natural abilities differ from individual to individual, and nowhere do they show up more than on hills. It is of course possible to walk up hills but many people find it easier to ride up almost anything in a low enough gear, even at little more than walking pace. On longer and perhaps less steep hills you will find it is uncomfortable to try to go much faster than your

natural speed and probably tedious to go much slower. If you are with companions whose natural speeds are different it is best for each to travel at their chosen pace and to meet again at the top (or at intervals on a mountain pass).

It's quite easy to get very hungry and thirsty when cycling. The cooling and evaporating effect of the passing air means that in warm weather you can be steadily perspiring quite heavily without realizing it. Plain water and some simple carbohydrates such as fruit bars or biscuits are best for immediate replenishment. It's better to have fairly frequent stops for small meals and snacks than infrequent large ones.

Taking a bike with you

You may on occasion want to travel further afield than you can manage comfortably by bicycle, but would like to have the bike available at your destination. It's possible to take it by rail, road, air or sea.

Rail travel with a bicycle ought to be simple – but it often isn't. In Britain there are some lines on which you can take a bike with no restriction, free of charge. You just put your bike in the guard's van. On others you have to make a reservation for bicycle space (for a fee); on these services – which include most of the high speed mainline routes – bicycle space may be restricted, and may not be available on all trains. On a few lines there is no provision at all for cycle carriage. British Rail produce a booklet, their so-called *British Rail guide to better biking* which gives more detail. When taking a bicycle by train it is wise to remove any detachable accessories such as bags, pumps, bottles and lights, and to secure the bicycle so that it cannot fall over (but without locking it to anything).

A few coach companies, mainly in Scotland, will carry a very small number of bicycles if pre-booked: enquire locally. The most usual way of transporting a bike by road is by car. Some estate cars will quite easily accept a couple of bikes without any dismantling or merely with the front wheel removed. It's worth using an old sheet or piece of plastic to separate them, otherwise pedals and the like can become entangled. On other cars some type of rack is needed. Roof racks are available to hold bicycles right way up (often with the front wheel removed and carried

Rear mounting car racks can reduce wind resistance at speed and noise. Rear mounted car racks are also very compact.

separately) or upside down. Upside-down racks are usually quicker to load and unload but may require a lot of adjustment if you are carrying bicycles of different sizes. You also have to take care to avoid entangling brake cables and suchlike. Because bicycle wheelbases are all nearly the same, a right-way-up rack may be an easier solution for bicycles of differing size. Rear-mounted racks are also available, usually to carry only one or two bikes. Make sure that any rack is firmly fitted, and that the bikes are firmly fixed to it. Also bicycles can affect the car's susceptibility to side winds and will increase fuel consumption. It's also wise to restrict top speed.

Most airlines will accept bicycles, either within the baggage allowance or for a small fee.

(Above) In cycle sport bikes are usually carried on the roof of team cars. A large number can be accommodated. (Right) The seasonal snow tunnel on the descent of the Col du Glandon in the French Alps.

Cycle sport

Audax riding/Randonnées

The majority of people, including a large number of ordinary cyclists, cannot understand why anyone should want to involve themselves in racing. Hills are things to be avoided if possible, and the thought of training, of actually 'making it hurt' in order to improve one's competitive edge, is anathema to them.

On the other hand, a substantial proportion of experienced cycling tourists, some of whom enjoy 'hard-riding' or 'pass-storming' – riding over mountains – find themselves craving some further challenge, without necessarily wainting to commit themselves to the rigorous training regime that racing demands. Such cyclists are catered for by the *Randonnée*. Randonnées are organized rides, sometimes over set distances of 30–375 miles (50–600km), and sometimes based on a city to city itinerary. Riders can go in a group or solo, and must complete the distance within a set time.

Orginally Audax riding, as it is known, involved swimming, running, or walking a certain distance, or cycling 125 miles (200 km). In 1904 Henri Desgrange, who had founded the Tour de France the previous year, formulated the rules for the Audax Club Parisien, and organized events throughout France. The most famous – and most demanding – such ride is the Paris–Brest–Paris, which began as a road race – the distance of 750 miles (1200 km) must be completed within ninety hours, which means riding an average 200 miles (310 km) each day for nearly four days on a bike which must be equipped with lights and mudguards (fenders).

(Above) The London to Brighton randonnée start. Some 5,000 cyclists take part.

(Left) The muddy pavé of the Paris-Roubaix used by both the classic road-race and the randonnée. The rider is Italian Francesco Moser.

Riders carry check-cards, called 'carnets', which are stamped at control points along the route. Paris–Brest–Paris is held every four years and attracts hundreds of riders from all over Europe, Britain and the USA.

Another popular Randonnée is the Paris–Roubaix, which follows the bleak route through Northeastern France of the famous one-day classic road race. The ride covers a distance of 168 miles (272 km), and is composed of a gruelling string of country lanes, farm tracks and

ancient cobbled roads which are specially conserved for the events. Even in summer it rains frequently and the potholes are invariably full of water. The masochistic riders who survive the pounding from the 30 miles (50 km) of cobbles usually arrive exhausted and covered in mud.

In order to take part in Paris–Brest–Paris, riders must complete a qualifying ride of 380 miles (600 km) in forty hours. Audax UK was formed in 1976 to help prospective P–B–P participants qualify, and a 600 km ride from Windsor

A leisurely 1920s randonnée near London. With the motor car still an expensive luxury, the bike enjoyed great popularity.

to Chester and back was established. Audax UK (AUK) organizes over 200 rides throughout the country all year round. Rides are handled locally by regional coordinators and are advertized in the cycling press as well as in AUK's own publicity. In return for a small fee participants receive route details and check cards. Anyone can ride: it is not necessary to be a member of a club or association.

AUK has over 1,200 members and is affiliated to its French counterpart, through which riders have access to continental randonnées. Besides the P–B–P, there are some super long distance events such as Calais–Brindisi, which begins at the north eastern French port and and finishes 1200 miles (1920 km) away in the heel of Italy. AUK organizes some ultra long distance events, and in 1989 there was a new randonnée, the London to Edinburgh and back: 820 miles (1300 km) which must be completed within 96 hours. Members of AUK receive a quarterly journal containing news and reminiscences.

In the USA, there is an identical organization based in Syracuse, New York which is also affiliated to the Audax Club Parisien and the Randonneurs Mondiaux. They arrange a comprehensive programme of randonnées from 125 to 375 miles (200 to 600 km) in each of the sixteen cities where there is a regional coordinator. These stretch from Vancouver to Florida and include New York, San Francisco, and Lexington, Kentucky. Besides regional activities Audax USA organize package travel and accommodation for randonneurs wishing to participate in the Paris–Brest–Paris. They also produce a regular newsletter and an annual journal containing accounts of past rides.

In addition to the rides organized by Audax US there are a number of other cycle rides which, though not strictly randonnées, merit mention. The Tour of the Scioto River Valley (TOSRV) is a long established event held over two days. It attracts a complete range of cyclists, some of whom amble at their own pace, while others treat the event as a time trial, aiming to cover the two one-hundred mile stages as quickly as possible. The US 'Bikecentennial' ride is based on a 4250 mile (6800 km) coast-to-coast route that was established in the Bicentennial year. Although really a touring ride, such long distances demand a degree of determination and fitness that is not required for normal, shorter distance touring.

Besides the events over standard terrain, Audax also organize mountain randonnées, called *Brevets des grimpeurs*. The Bruges to Mont Ventoux finishes on the French mountain made famous by the Tour de France. The Tom Simpson memorial was established in memory of the English rider who collapsed and died on the Ventoux in 1967 Tour de France. The ride involves two laps of a circuit that goes round and over the mountain.

The US Bikecentennial organization have a coast-to-coast route of over 4,000 miles. Less demanding rides are also organized.

The Tommy Simpson memorial on Mont Ventoux, in memory of the English rider who died in 1967.

Cycling clubs can be well worth joining. Here is a club outing.

As well as events, Audax have also established 'Randonnées permanentes' which are fixed routes that may be ridden at any time. Riders receive details and a set of carnets which may be stamped in the usual way, but there are no time limits. (Part of the fun of Audax is in collecting carnets, stamps and certificates.)

Reliability trials

Most cycling clubs organize 'reliability trials' as part of their annual calendar. Such rides are non-competitive and take place during the winter months when the racing season is closed. Reliability trials are held over distances of 60–100 miles (100–160 km). A choice of three or four times is available within which the distance must be covered. Riders are set off in groups and are issued with check cards which are handed in at the control points. For cyclists who think they may want to go into racing one day but haven't yet decided, reliability trials are an excellent entrée into the club cycling world, which tends to be racing orientated, but which also has a strong social element. These events, and the weekly 'club-runs', provide an opportunity to meet other cyclists and hence to find out about the local racing scene.

Most clubs organize a handful of competitive events each year, which provide a good opportunity to try out some friendly racing. Cycling clubs are welcoming organizations, and their trials and club-runs are open to non-members regardless of whether they intend joining or not. Like randonnées reliability trials are usually advertized in the cycling press

Racing teams at the Crystal Palace track in the 1890s.
Note the banking and the five riders on the two inside bikes.

Cycle racing: track and road

In 1863, Pierre and Ernest Michaux began producing velocipedes in quantity and five years later the first recorded cycle race took place. It was held over a distance of 1200 metres, in the Parc St Cloud in Paris, and was won by James Moore, an Englishman. In 1869 Moore won an 83 mile (133 km) road race, the first of its kind, from Paris to Rouen, from among 325 starters, in a time of 10 hours and 25 minutes. Women rode the race too, and the first to reach Rouen was a Miss Turner, who called herself 'Miss America'.

As technological developments to the bicycle accelerated, so did the popularity of racing. By 1871 there was a professional class competing regularly in Britain, while in the USA the League of American Wheelmen was founded in 1880. By 1889 its membership had grown to 102 000, three times the membership of the US Cycling federation in 1987! Racing had begun in Boston in 1878, thirteen years before basketball was invented.

The development of road racing in Britain was hampered by poor quality roads, and was in any case killed-off in 1889 by a total ban on safety grounds. Hence the popularity of track racing in the last two decades of the century. By 1900 a slump in the cycle trade led to the closure of many tracks, and so the only other activity for racing men and women was time-trialling, which to this day remains the most popular, if inconspicuous branch of the sport in the UK.

In Europe, by contrast, road racing developed steadily with the aid of commercial sponsorship, and a programme of 'Classic' one-day and short stage racing, culminating in the big National Tours   was established early on in the century.

(Top left) Ladies' international indoor track race in London in 1896. The display of legs allowed by the costumes was considered most immodest.

(Above) Boys will be boys. Victorian racing stars Dan Albone and Monty Holbein (in carrier) go back to school.

(Left) The Herne Hill cycle track in 1895. The track had a wooden surface and was the scene of many important early races.

Tactics

Over the years, road racing has developed into three distinct branches; the *Criterium*, the *single-day race* and the *stage race*, which consists of a series of races, or 'stages', held over a number of consecutive days. But although all three activities demand very different kinds of skill and abilities, they have one thing in common: all are highly tactical, to the extent that a rider of lesser physical prowess can more than compensate by knowing how to 'read' a race, and consequently how and when to attack – to try and ride away from the front of the main bunch of riders, either alone or in a group.

At the beginning of a race, the group of riders will stay together, and if the course is flat they may well stay together for the whole race. On such a course the big men – the sprinters – will organize a breakaway with the aid of their team-mates. The team-mates – or *domestiques* as the lesser members of a team are known on the continent – will take it in turn to ride in front, while the sprinter shelters in their slipstream – conserving his strength for as long as possible. Then, with about 200 metres to go, the team-mates will peel away and the sprinter will charge for the line.

By taking it in turns to ride for a few seconds on the front, then sheltering behind the line of riders, a much higher tempo can be maintained than a rider could manage alone. Thus a race can rarely be won by a rider simply going off the front and leaving the bunch behind for the duration (although this does occasionally happen, especially if the bunch underestimate a rider's ability, as they did when Darryl Webster, a first-year British pro, stayed away on his own for 120 miles (192 km) in the Nissan Tour of Ireland in 1988).

A rider breaks away from the bunch. Attempts to 'go solo' rarely achieve ultimate success. The pursuing bunch has the advantage of being able to work together to recover the lost ground. Occasionally however, they can miscalculate.

If a race takes in a few hills or as is often the case, is based on a 6–8 mile (4–13 km) circuit with a hill in the middle, tactics will be quite different. Hills always split the bunch, because there will be good climbers in there who can take advantage of the sprinters' poor climbing ability. As the race moves up the hill, the climbers will attack, open up a gap, and then try to stay away.

On the next lap, if they can, they will do the same thing again, and so in this way will try to keep away until the finish; they know that if caught they will not be able to win in a sprint to the line.

When riders form a break they may not necessarily have a team-mate with them. In this case they will have to work with their opponents. This complicates the strategy because each rider knows that if he works harder on the front than the others, they will take advantage of his tiredness at the finish, since the co-operation between them is only temporary. In such a situation a rider may even refuse to do his fair share of work on the front. But if all the riders in the break then refuse their fair share, they will all slow down, and then risk being caught by the bunch. This dilemma can cause riders to panic. If a break has been away for 50–60 miles (80–95 km), the last thing they want is to have all their effort wasted. So sometimes a rider will try a sudden escape on his own, using the element of surprise to get away. If he can stay away he might win, but if he is caught by the break his

Spectacular crashes can occur in road races when a large number of riders are tightly bunched. Here at least twelve are involved.

chances are diminished because of the extra energy he has expended.

If a break goes away with two or more riders from the same team, the other members of the team will use 'blocking tactics' in the bunch. This involves them riding at the front and trying to slow the pace, so that the break can maximize its lead. One can see this happening in the early, flat stages of the Tour de France, when for example members of the Dutch Panasonic or Superconfex teams may ride in a group at the head of the race. If a rider tries to jump away to the break, they will immediately sit in front of him and block his escape until he is engulfed by the bunch again.

In professional road racing riders take it in turns at the front of a bunch. This makes it possible for a much higher tempo to be maintained than would otherwise be the case.

Team organization

In pro racing, teams are organized hierarchically, based on a system of stars and domestiques. The star rider or team leader is the one with proven ability and on whom the hopes of the manager and sponsors are pinned. It is the domestiques' duty to serve and facilitate the progress of the leader by employing blocking tactics and by pacing him – 'leading-out' – in sprint finishes. Additionally, the domestique will be required to carry water bottles from the team support car up

The Gazelle/Vredestein team. Most riders in a large team are domestiques and their job is to help their star riders. Occasionally however, a domestique will enjoy the limelight.

(Left) A Tour de France rider is illegally 'towed' by a back-up car on a hard mountain stage.

to the leader, and to pace him back to the bunch if he has to stop for a puncture or mechanical trouble. In doing all this, the domestique must subordinate his personal aspirations to those of the leader. Many riders are content with this role and are none the less respected for it. They may eventually get a taste of glory, as did Sean Yates, the British rider who won a time trial stage of the 1988 Tour de France.

Criteriums

Criteriums are held on a short, usually flat, circuit, often as little as half a mile or one kilometre round. The course is made up of city streets, closed off to traffic, with several sharp corners to be negotiated. A race might last sixty laps. The pace is fast and furious, with accelerations on the straight followed almost immediately by hard braking at corners. Riders constantly attack, and try to get a break going, often alone, as it is hard for a break of, say, six to work effectively on such a tight circuit.

Unlike single day and stage races, criteriums provide a good spectacle, since the riders will pass every minute or two. Because of this, the spectator can monitor the development of the race in a way that is impossible with a long road event. In the pro calendar criteriums are mostly held in a three or four-week period after the Tour de France in July. Riders can earn a lot of appearance money for these races, and this is not unconnected with the fact that their sponsors' publicity on their shorts and jerseys, will be seen sixty times by each spectator.

The professional season: single day races and the great national tours

After a winter of speed skating, cyclo-cross, distance riding or cross-country skiing, the professional season begins in February with a training camp in California or the South of France, and this will be followed by 'pre-season' races such as the Monaco Grand Prix or the Tour du Haut Var. Then comes a string of mostly single-day classics, beginning with Het Volk, promoted by the eponymous Belgian newspaper. This is followed by one of the most prestigious races: Paris–Nice, which was won a record seven times in a row from 1982–88 by the Irishman, Sean Kelly.

The influx of English-speaking riders has been the abiding feature of pro-racing in the 1980s, and their presence has done much to shake up a scene which had become moribund under the dominance of Eddy Merckx in the 1970s and Bernard Hinault in the first half of the 80s. In the 1985 Tour de France, the American Greg LeMond was lying second to team leader Bernard Hinault, who was riding with a fractured nose. Hinault wanted his fifth Tour win to equal the total of Jacques Anquetil and Eddy Merckx before him. LeMond wanted, and was in a position to take the lead from the suffering Hinault, but was prevented from doing so by the team coach, who insisted LeMond support Hinault.

The following year, Hinault had promised to help LeMond win in exchange for the sacrifice he had made in 1985, but as the race progressed it became clear that Hinault was prepared to break his promise in pursuit of a record sixth win. The La Vie Claire team split into a European faction which supported Hinault and an American faction consisting of Andy Hampsten and LeMond. Behind the surface camaraderie Hinault and LeMond continued to battle it out until LeMond eventually won by a margin of some two minutes. Although LeMond was subsequently fêted by the Tour organizers, the whole episode symbolises the ambivalence with which English-speaking riders were regarded in what had until then been an almost solely European affair.

For some riders the one-day classics are treated as training for the more demanding stage races and national tours that take place in spring and mid-summer. But for many, the early classics, especially Paris–Nice, Paris–Roubaix and the Belgian races (Flèche–Wallone, Liège–Bastogne–Liège and Ghent–Wevelgem) are sufficiently pretigious to make a speciality. The 168 miles (272 km) of Paris–Roubaix is in many ways the hardest of the classics. The absence of hills is more than compensated for by the narrow country lanes, the treacherous farm-tracks and 20–30 miles (30–50 km) of ancient cobbled roads (*pavé*) over which the race winds its way. Although held in April, the weather is frequently wet and inevitably there are many crashes on the slippery cobbles. Nevertheless the race is run-off at an average speed of 26–27 mph.

Although these races are early in the season, they are every bit as hard in their way as the big tours: the weather is often bad, and the courses, (with the exception of Paris–Roubaix) are peppered with short, sharp climbs up slippery cobbled lanes. Because most of them are one-day races, rides can go all-out in the knowledge that they have not got to get up and race again the next day. A heavy programme of early classics can tire a rider sufficiently to diminish his chances in the big tours. It says a lot for the early classics' prestige that riders are prepared to make this sacrifice.

In contrast to riders who revel in the Belgian races, are those who plan their entire season around the Tour de France, foregoing all the hardest classics in order to peak in July. Lucian van Impe succesfully employed this strategy in 1976. But such a practice does not endear riders to their sponsors who want their products advertized in as many races as possible.

Besides the different types of race, the riders themselves fall naturally into certain ability groups. Just as each sport has its specialists so cycling has its sprinters, climbers and time-trial-lists as well as those who excel on all types of terrain. A large stage-race like the Tour de France is routed over an immensely varied terrain and landscape in order to test the skills of the different kinds of riders.

Pure sprinters like Jean-Paul van Poppel or Eric Vanderaerden are prominent in the early, flat stages of the Tour, where they can jump away from the bunch over the last 200 metres of the race, accelerate to 50 mph (80 kph) in seconds, and take the stage. In the 1988 Tour, van Poppel

Riders' build. Extreme right big sprinter Vanderaerden, behind him lighter climber Theunisse and all-round ability Lauritzen. Tour de Trump 1989.

won three stages in this manner. But sprinters are invariably big, strong, heavy men, whose weight serves them well on the flat, but slows them down as soon as they hit the mountains. Suddenly they have got perhaps an extra 28 lbs (13 kg) of weight, albeit muscle, to haul up 10 miles (16 km) of 1 in 7 (14%) gradient.

Climbers, by contrast, are always light and usually small, and although 'weaker' than the average sprinter, have a higher strength to weight ratio, which gives them the advantage up hills. Robert Millar of Scotland, the Spaniard Pedro Delgado and Colombian Luis Herrera all excel in the mountains, and just as the best sprinters come from Belgium and Holland, so it is no coincidence that the best climbers come mostly from mountainous areas. In both cases they will have worked their way up through the amateur ranks in a sport where the nature of the local terrain helps to determine which type of rider will enjoy national, and thence international success.

There are always exceptions to this rule: Steven Rooks, who was mountains champion in the 1988 Tour de France, hails from Holland. But Irishman Sean Kelly is the exception par excellence. Until 1982 Kelly was known as, and believed himself to be, a pure sprinter. Then from 1982–88 he won Paris–Nice every year. In the process Kelly's abilities were transformed, and he changed from being 'just' a sprinter to

Irishman Sean Kelly, whose abilities were transformed from pure sprinter to the most consistent all-rounder in the world.

become the most consistent all-rounder in the world. In 1984 he won 33 races, including Paris–Roubaix and Liège–Bastogne–Liège, and by 1988 his climbing ability had improved so much that he won the Tour of Spain, the hilliest of the big three national tours. In the mean time, Kelly has retained his sprinting power almost undimmed.

As the season progresses, the single-day races are gradually interspersed with stage races. In March the Catalan week, the Tour of Reggio Calabria and the Belgian three days of La Panne, although not unduly tiring give riders a chance to prepare themselves for the particular demands of stage racing. Besides being a good all-rounder, the successful stage racer needs to be able to recover quickly after an exhausting day in the mountains. Unlike in the one-day classics, he will have to get up and do the whole thing all over again the next day, and again the day after that, continuing in this fashion for perhaps four or five days in a row. That kind of regime takes its toll on big riders, who need longer to recover after a stage, and hence riders of moderate build tend to be best suited to stage racing. (Pure climbers tend to lack the strength to time-trial well, and hence lose valuable seconds in those crucial stages.) All the Tour de France winners of recent years have been of a medium build.

Three portraits of great road racing champions. (Far left) The legendary Eddy Merckx. (Centre) French star Laurent Fignon. (Right) American ace Greg LeMond, twice winner of the Tour de France.

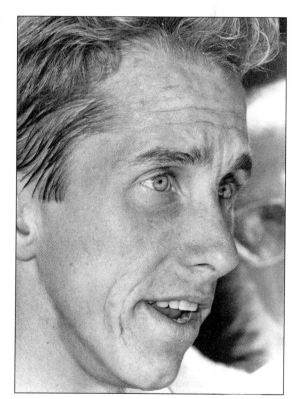

The Vuelta d'Espana and the Giro d'Italia: National Passions

The Spanish Vuelta, shortest of the big three national tours with approximately twenty stages, is nevertheless quite hard enough to test the most able of riders. There are more climbs than in the other tours, and this makes it very hard for riders who are used to a preponderance of flat stages. Although foreigners (Hinault in 1983, Kelly in 1988) have won the tour, it tends to favour the Spanish teams, which are composed predominantly of smaller men who can climb well. In 1989, for example, the Vuelta was won by Pedro Delgado, and the next four places were taken by Spanish or Spanish-speaking riders.

Not surprisingly Spaniards want a Spanish winner for their tour. In the 1985 Vuelta, their hopes were upset by Robert Millar who won several stages. But before he could consolidate his lead, Spanish riders conspired to block his moves and thus prevented him from winning. In the 1987 Giro d'Italia the Irish winner Stephen Roche was also victimized for upstaging their national hero.

The Italians also want a national winner for their race, so much so that the organizers will design the race to suit their current in-form star. In 1983 sprint bonuses were introduced in order to help Giuseppe Saronni, a sprinter and the then Professional World Champion, to win. The following year, despite the preponderance of mountains in the peninsula, a largely flat Giro course was designed to facilitate the victory of

(Above) Pedro Delgado, Spanish winner of both the Vuelta and Tour de France. (Right) Low temperatures and high climbs in the Giro d'Italia.

Francesco Moser. This is not to undervalue Moser's ability as a rider: he has won Paris–Roubaix three times, the World Championship Road Race and numerous classics, as well as two world track records.

But Moser is no climber, and had never won the Giro in his long career. One of the flattest Giro courses ever gave Moser a winning chance, but in the end Hinault triumphed by seven seconds on the last stage, during which he was subjected to a barrage of insults, beer cans and

(Left) The Passo Stelvio on the Giro d'Italia: hard going. (Above) Stephen Roche, domestique turned Giro d'Italia winner and also winner of the Tour de France.

tin tacks. The same treatment was meted out to Stephen Roche in 1987. As a *domestique*, albeit a 'super' one, Roche was expected to serve his leader in the Carrera team, Roberto Visentini. But Visentini failed to show good form and Roche's clear superiority allowed him to move into a winning position. Despite the refusal of the team to work for Roche, he went on to win in a hail of missiles. Later that year Roche also won the Tour de France and the World Professional Road Race Championships, one of only three riders ever to do so.

The Tour de France

The Tour de France is one of the great events on the international sporting calendar and in 1989 with extensive coverage by television was watched by some 10 million people. It is front page news in France, Belgium and Holland and in its sheer scale and in the demands made on the riders, the tour truly merits the description of epic. Three weeks in duration, with some 20 stages and a length of over 2000 miles (3200 km), covering terrain varying from flat countryside to 2500 metre mountains to the boulevards of Paris, the tour is indeed a supreme test of a rider's fitness and character. So punishing are some of the hot mountain stages, where a one in ten gradient is not unknown, that a rider will consume up to 9000 calories, drink several gallons of water and still end the day up to sixteen pounds lighter.

In recent years European racing, and the Tour de France in particular, has been enlivened by the challenge of English speaking riders. In 1986 Greg LeMond became the first such rider and the first American to win the Tour, bringing to fruition a process that had begun a decade earlier, in 1973. That year Jonathan Boyer left California and joined the ACBB, a Parisian cycling club sponsored by Peugeot from which a number of English speakers have launched successful pro careers. Boyer turned pro in 1977 and finally rode the Tour, the first American to do so, in 1980.

Since then Andy Hampsten, Eric Heiden, Davis Phinney, Roy Knickman, Ron Kiefel, Greg LeMond and others have enjoyed success,

either with European teams or with the American 7-Eleven squad, which has competed prominently in the United States and Europe. In 1989, after a serious shooting accident, appendicitis and poor form laid him off for two and a half years, an optimistic LeMond returned to contest the Tour again.

The Tour spans the first three weeks of July, and to taste its excitement let us follow the 1989 event. This tour was shorter than usual, consisting of 21 stages with a total distance of 2040 miles (3260 km). But although shorter, the race was one of the hilliest for years. It was sensational not just for LeMond's come-back, but because the pre-race favourite, 1988 winner Pedro Delgado, seriously jeopardized his chances of winning in the first two days of the race, leaving it wide open with five or six potential victors.

The first stage is a 'prologue' individual time-trial, in which riders are set off at one minute intervals to ride against the clock. The winner of the Tour is the rider who completes the race in the shortest overall time, and one function of the prologue TT is to establish an initial race order based on riders' individual times. This cannot be done from a bunch (péloton) sprint finish, where 150 riders might cross the line, all within

(Right) An early stage start of the Tour de France. Riders would wear spare around their shoulders as punctures were common.

(Left) The year is 1934 and Antonin Magne celebrates winning the Tour.

two seconds of each other. When the race reaches the mountains, time gaps will really open up, but until then the time-trial serves to create an order.

Incredibly Delgado, warming up before his test, lost sight of the time and when he eventually reported to the starting box, the clock had already counted away nearly three minutes on him. Instead of finishing 26th, as he would had he started on time, he came last in 198th place, a potentially disastrous 2 min 54 sec behind the winner, Eric Breukink.

Despite this, commentators were quick to point out that Delgado had won the '88 Tour by a margin of seven minutes, so all was not necessarily lost. But worse was to come. Stages two and three were both held on the following day, with a short 85 mile (135 km) road race in the morning, and a team time-trial (TT) in the afternoon. Just as the individual TT establishes an order of the individual riders, so the team TT serves the same purpose for teams, since the Tour yields a winning team, as well as a rider.

In the third stage Delgado's Reynolds squad came last as direct result of Delgado 'blowing up' – running out of energy. His consequent

(Top right) A large television monitor shows what is happening elsewhere. (Right) The advertisers come to town. (Opposite, left) An injured rider after a crash. (Opposite, top right) Latest policeman's transport. (Opposite, bottom right) The prizes: the leaders' jerseys, presented after each stage. The jerseys represent every rider's dream.

inability to keep up with his team-mates forced them to slow dramatically half-way round the 29 mile (46 km) course, so that Delgado could stay in contact. In an event where teams drill themselves meticulously in order to ride in tight formation all the way round, taking turns on the front to keep the pace high, such lapses are disastrous. By the end of stage three, the Reynolds team had slumped to bottom place, and Delgado's personal deficit had grown to a massive 9 min 57 sec behind Acacio da Silva, the new leader.

As the race moved out of Luxembourg, across Belgium and into north-eastern France, da Silva retained his overall lead for one more day before losing it on stage five to LeMond in the second individual time-trial over 46 miles (73 km). This time Delgado was punctual and came in second, only 38 seconds behind LeMond, to dramatically improve his position from 197th to 28th, though this still left him nearly seven minutes down on LeMond's overall time. Also in close contention was Laurent Fignon, two times Tour winner and French hope, lying second overall, a mere five seconds behind the American. These details, however, were overshadowed by LeMond's dramatic return after nearly three years out. He had stormed through the last 16 miles (25 km) of the stage, showing the brilliant

Pedro Delgado hard at work to make up for lost time. His mysterious late arrival at the prologue TT had just jeopardized his chances but he fought his way back into contention.

The Tour sweeps up into the mountains. Da Silva leads. Heavily built sprinters now start to fall back in the overall classification.

Torment in the mountains. An exhausted rider is sponged down. Riders have to be superbly fit in these conditions.

time-trialling skill which could eventually prove decisive in this the 86th Tour.

For the next three days the race moved from Rennes, down the western side of France through Bordeaux to the Pyrenees, and LeMond retained the yellow jersey of race leader, with Fignon still at five seconds, and Sean Kelly leading the points competition. Besides being a consistent rider from season to season and from race to race, Kelly also finishes regularly in the top ten places of a stage. The prize for this is the green points jersey and by the end of the Tour Kelly had won it a record six times.

Stage nine, from Labastide to Pau, was won by Kelly's team-mate and fellow Irishman Martin Earley. On stage ten, 82 miles (136 km) from Cauteret to Superbagnères, 1770 metres up in the Pyrenees, the climbers at last came out of the bunch to attack the four big passes, including the final climb to the finish. This time the stage fell to the Scot Robert Millar, who not only led over the first three climbs, but also beat Delgado to the line in a furious sprint. In so doing Millar settled two scores. Firstly, he beat the Spaniard whose team had blocked his attempts to win the 1985 Vuelta, and secondly he made amends for losing the mountainous 14th stage of the '88 Tour to the Italian Massimo Ghirotto, after a marshal sent Millar off course when he was leading Ghirotto with 100 metres to go. LeMond came up the mountain in a group with Fignon, but Fignon attacked again and again until LeMond could no longer respond. Lemond eventually finished the stage in ninth place, 12 seconds behind the Frenchman, who now led by seven seconds. Delgado, meanwhile, had forced his way back to fourth overall.

The race now left the Pyrenees and crossed the Midi to the Alps, Fignon holding on to his lead for the next four stages to stage 15, a 24 mile (39 km) individual mountain TT from Gap to Orcières. If there were any doubts about how LeMond would fare in a mountain TT, given his shaky performance in the Pyrenees, they were now dispelled. Whatever LeMond lacked in climbing ability, he more than made up for in time-trialling skill. He rode up the first climb of the Nanse, and thence via a steep, winding descent to the second, the plateau of Orcières–Merlette, to finish fifth to Dutchman Steven Rooks, 47 seconds ahead of 10th-placed Laurent Fignon.

Stage 16, from Gap to Briançon, provided a stiff Alpine test of 110 miles (174 km) with two major climbs. After an early break of 18 men got away, a chasing group formed at 56 miles (90 km) at the foot of the Col de Vars. Fignon, LeMond, Rooks and French champion Charly Mottet gradually caught and dropped the eighteen one by one. During all this, the group also constantly attacked LeMond, in a systematic drive to wear him down, as Fignon had done at Superbagnères. But LeMond kept pulling them back, and stayed with the group over the 2360m of the Col d'Izoard, with its final 3 miles (5 km) of 1 in 10 gradient. Not only did he retain his

The Col du Galibier at 2640 metres high is one of the very hardest mountains on the Tour. In 1989 both Delgado and Fignon rode well on this very tough and demanding stage.

lead, he extended it slightly to 53 seconds.

But on stage 17, 101 miles (160 km) from Briançon to l'Alpe d'Huez, LeMond paid for all his enforced counterattacking of the previous day. Over three of the highest and hardest mountains in the Tour – the 2640m of the Col du Galibier, the Col de la Croix de Fer and l'Alpe d'Huez – Fignon again attacked and pounced on LeMond, Delgado and Delgado's team mate Abelardo Rondon as soon as they tried to escape. Fignon regained the yellow jersey with 26 seconds in hand, but Delgado too was right back in contention, outsprinting Fignon on the line to finish 2 min 28 sec down overall.

On stage 18, the hottest day of the Tour, Fignon extended his lead to 50 seconds. Well aware of LeMond's superior time-trialling ability, he reckoned on needing at least thirty seconds lead to be reasonably sure of winning the Tour. He chose the hottest day of the year to improve his position, hoping to capitalize on LeMond's imperfect record in the mountains.

On stage 19 of the Tour, the fifth and final day in the Alps, it was LeMond who sprinted to victory in a race between Marino Lejaretta of Spain

and the three other main overall contenders, Fignon, Delgado and Gert-Jan Theunisse. Although Fignon retained his 50-second advantage, LeMond had proved he could climb and win a mountain stage. Not only that, he could also descend fearlessly, and even attacked at 60 mph (96 kph) on the six mile (10 km) drop from the Col du Granier.

The penultimate stage 20, a short run from Aix-les-Bains to l'Isle d'Abeau was flat and uneventful. Kelly was third in the bunch sprint,

(Below) Greg LeMond (in yellow jersey), not a natural climber, hangs on as the pace hots up. Excited spectators are a feature of the Tour.

(Below) Charley Mottet rode with LeMond on stage 16 and still had every chance of winning the Tour. Mottet was with the RMO team.

consolidating his lead in the points competition. And so to stage 21, the finale into Paris. In past years this last stage has invariably been a perfunctory affair: a demonstration event for the dense, cheering crowds on the Champs Elysées. The race leader will have built up an inviolable lead of two minutes or more, and has only to sit tight in the bunch while his team-mates carefully protect him.

But 1989 was different. It was to be an individual TT over a mere 16 miles (25 km) from the Palace of Versailles to the Champs Elysées. True, Fignon had a substantial lead over LeMond, and many doubted whether the latter could win back that amount of time over such a short distance. On the other hand, the two men had already exchanged the yellow jersey three times, and it seemed just possible it could happen again. As race leader, Fignon was under pressure, while LeMond had nothing to lose.

LeMond set off at 2.12 pm on a low profile bike with rear disc wheel and triathlon handlebars which give the rider a more comfortable position without sacrificing the low profile. Two minutes later Fignon started his ride on a similar machine equipped with standard bars and two disc wheels. But while LeMond quickly settled into a rhythm on the flat course, pedalling smoothly and steering a clean line through the bends, Fignon was struggling to control his bike and seemed unable to settle down into his ride. This may have been due to the front disc wheel, which makes handling much more difficult, especially if there is a wind. Ironically, the aero-

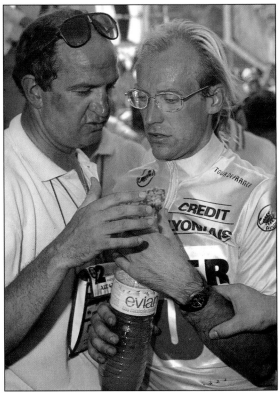

dynamic advantage that the front disc is intended to give was more than cancelled out by the extra distance Fignon added to the course by weaving around all over the road. At 7 miles (11.5 km) LeMond had gained a dramatic 21 seconds on his rival and rode on relentlessly to win the Tour – by the margin of eight seconds, the closest ever finish in the race's history.

Delgado, third at 3 min 34 sec, was left to consider what might have been had he avoided his disastrous start. Sean Kelly won both points

Although he was troubled by an incipient saddle-boil, and was apparently uneasy with two disc wheels, Laurent Fignon still rode his best ever time-trial on the finale into Paris. LeMond however rode even better. (Above) Fignon is consoled after the disaster.

and Catch sprint competition, the latter being for intermediate sprints or 'primes', held along the course each day.

(Above) Sean Kelly, who won both points and Catch sprint competitions, at speed.

(Left) A rock steady Greg LeMond on his final time-trial, the world's fastest ever at 54kmh. It gave him an historic victory and his second win of the Tour de France. Two years earlier he had nearly bled to death in a shooting accident.

The Tour Féminin

Unfortunately, cycle racing, particularly on the road, is a male-dominated sport, but in recent years an increasing number of women have become involved and the amateur Tour de France Féminin, which began in 1984 and was won that year by the American Marianne Martin, has encouraged this process.

The 1989 edition consisted of eleven stages, run on the same roads and on the same days as the men's race so that spectators could enjoy both events. With a fifth stage of 123 miles (196 km) and some hard climbs, the women proved themselves to be every bit as courageous and determined as the men, if not as fast, and the race has proved far more popular with spectators than the organizers had presumed. Indeed, if they had bothered to research the history of women's racing they would have discovered a thriving professional track scene in the 1880s. Stars like the Algerian Aboukaia and her French partner Reillo won the British National tandem championships in 1989 in front of a sell-out crowd of 12000 on the track at Wood Green, North London. Recently, the Tour has been dominated by Jeannie Longo of France, who won five consecutive stages in 1989 to win the Tour for the third year running.

Debbie Shumway, the American rider, on the Tour Féminin. Although the riders on this tour are amateurs they enjoy the same facilities as the men and their standards are rapidly rising.

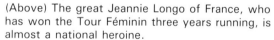

(Above) The great Jeannie Longo of France, who has won the Tour Féminin three years running, is almost a national heroine.

(Top right) A German lady rider takes some liquid refreshment.

(Left) British rider Maria Blower riding hard on a time-trial during the 1989 Tour Féminin. The tour is proving increasingly popular with spectators.

(Bottom right) Great Britain's Clare Greenwood took a creditable 16th place on the 1988 Tour Feminin. Great Britain have not yet fielded their strongest team in this event.

Racing in Ireland, Britain and the USA

In the last decade professional racing has flourished in the English-speaking countries. Two things have contributed to this state of affairs. Firstly, the televizing of races and the promotion of events, specifically for television by such specialist companies as Sport for Television. Secondly, the success on the continent of British, Irish, American and Canadian riders has certainly helped to invigorate the racing in their home countries.

In Ireland the Nissan Classic tour, and in Britain the Kelloggs' Tour and the Wincanton Classic are now sufficiently well-established and prestigious to attract the World's top stars, not least those natives who come home to ride them. In the USA the Tour of Texas, and the one day Core States Championship have become well established. The latter is a particular draw for European riders because the prize list of $105 000 is more than twice that of Europe's biggest one day race, the Paris–Roubaix, where $43 000 was on offer in 1987. In 1989 a brand new race, the Trump Tour, was held in the Eastern USA. The Tour was sponsored by multi-millionaire property developer Donald Trump, and it too attracted a world-class field.

Besides these major events the home-based pros have a full programme of smaller national races, and they will be in action every week from March to October. Next to all this activity is a thriving amateur scene with local, regional and national organizers providing a structured programme of road races for riders of all abilities. In

(Opposite) A helicopter hovers over riders in the 1989 Kelloggs' Tour. The Kelloggs' Tour is prestigious enough to attract world stars.

(Above) Riders stream through Westminster, past the Houses of Parliament and under the tower of Big Ben during the Kelloggs' Tour.

(Right) Robert Millar, a quiet Scottish rider, won the 1989 Kelloggs' Tour. Millar rode for the Peugeot team.

Britain there are three, and in the USA four, senior rider categories, with additional ones for juveniles, juniors, veterans and women. Senior riders start in categories three or four, and must accumulate points to move up a grade, which usually takes a season. First category racing is a serious and highly competitive pursuit, and a number of top amateurs, some of whom may be trying for Olympic selection, train and race full-time with the support of their clubs and families. Some turn professional, much to the chagrin of the national coach, but there is always new blood moving up through the ranks.

Although spectators cannot be party to all the

(Above right) The Tour de Trump hits Baltimore. North American riders have in recent years challenged the general European domination of cycle sport.

(Left) Riders cross the famous bridge in Newcastle during the Wincanton Classic. This race now attracts top international stars.

secret pacts and temporary alliances that are made in a road race, nor can they necessarily always follow the complex moves and counter-moves, road racing has a direct appeal which other branches of the sport do not enjoy. By comparison, the track disciplines can seem

monotonous and arcane. Road racing by contrast is heroic and spectacular, with its massed bunch sprints, nail-biting climbs and 60 mph (96 kph) descents.

While television has done much to bring racing to a wide general public, the best place to watch a stage of the Tour de France is three-quarters of the way up a mountain pass. A good position will permit a spectator to see the riders moving up through the hairpin bends lower down, before they come past at about one-third their normal racing speed. Many people take a picnic and make a day of it and it is necessary to arrive early to get a good position.

The Tour of Texas, 1989. (Far left) A skyscraper dwarfs riders in Fort Worth. (Above) Lady riders in the Frio canyon. This tour is one of only four major international tours for women. (Left) Canadian Alex Stieda, winner of the men's tour and first North American to wear the yellow jersey in the Tour de France. Stieda rode for the 7-eleven team, a pioneer of professional racers out of the USA.

The Track

Track racing took off in the 1880s, partly because the quality of roads was so poor that racing on them was virtually impossible.

The last twenty years of the nineteenth century were the golden age of track racing, and nowhere more so than in the USA, where riders from all over Europe and North America flocked to compete, drawn by the rich prize lists. August Zimmerman became the first World champion in 1893, and his rival, Major Taylor, the first black champion of any professional sport, in 1899. Despite the difficulties and restrictions Taylor faced through racial prejudice and the segregation of the sport, he eventually went on to become one of the most succesful riders ever, sometimes earning per day twice what his father earned in a year.

Track racing remained a rich and very popular sport until a combination of circumstances, including the Wall Street crash, led to its rapid decline in 1929. In Britain the track has always enjoyed a small following of enthusiasts, and

has produced a few notable riders such as Reg Harris, who won the British sprint title when in his fifties! In 1980 and '86 Tony Doyle won the World Pro Pursuit Championship, and this title was taken again in 1989 by Colin Sturgess. Sally Hodge won the 1988 World Points Race.

In the USA, Sue Novara and Sheila Young-Ochowicz won silver and gold respectively in the 1976 World Sprint Championships. The success of the US team in the 1984 Olympics was soured by the blood-doping scandal that engulfed them. Blood-doping involves taking a pint of a competitor's blood and storing it several weeks before the competition. The blood is reinjected before the event, in order to increase the oxygen carrying capacity of the blood stream by up to ten percent. Although not illegal at the time, it was felt to be, at the very least, unsporting, and the incident clouded the track competition.

Track racing divides into two main areas; the numerous disciplines such as sprinting, pursuiting, time-trialling, motor-paced and points racing for which there are pro and amateur competitions; and the winter six-day events which until recently, were strictly professional affairs. The Olympic specification track or velodrome is a 333.33 metres circuit made of hardwood planks with steep banking at each end and shallower banking on the straights. Some six-day tracks are as little as 200 metres round while many more may be bigger with little or no banking. The latter are usually open-air with a concrete or tarmac surface.

Sprinting

The classic track race is the paired sprint in which two riders are pitted against each other. It is perhaps the purest, most tactical of any cycle race. As we have seen earlier, an individual in a road race can rarely just ride off the front of the bunch and win, and the same applies to track sprinting. In fact the easiest way to win is to come from behind, and hence that is where both riders want to be (until the last 200 metres) – so much so that they draw lots to determine who will go in front at the start. The winner is decided on the best of three heats, each being over three laps. The rider who draws to go in front must stay there until one lap has been completed.

After the first lap the front rider will do everything he can to force his opponent to take the lead, including stopping on the banking (if he goes backwards, however, the race must be restarted). The rider behind will be equally determined to stay where he is: ideally he wants to ride in his opponent's slipstream until the very end.

With 200 metres to go the clock is started and the race springs to life. If one rider is still in front he will sprint hard and try to stay away for the next eleven seconds. If he is clever he will have ridden down off the banking to gain acceleration at the start of his effort. But the rider behind not only has the front man's slipstream, he also has the element of surprise. As long as he can stay with the front man when he accelerates he should be able to come past at the last moment.

(Far left) A velodrome in the USA. There is sharp banking at each end of the track and shallow banking on the straights. (Top left) A high speed crash is taking place in a ladies' sprint race. The helmets may soon be useful. Note the front wheel buckling under the strain. (Bottom left) A view of the shallower banking on the straight at the Leicester velodrome in the UK.

Tremendous stresses are placed on sprint bikes as their riders force them from five to 40 mph (eight to 64 kmh) in the last nine or ten seconds of the race. To withstand this strain sprint bikes are built with stiffer tubing, and round forkblades instead of the usual oval. They will have steel handlebars and stem, since, in the process of forcing his legs round, the rider pulls almost as hard on the bars as he pushes on the pedals; alloy bars tend to snap. The need for a stiff and responsive machine extends to the wheels, which will be built with large-flange hubs to reduce the length of the spokes between hub and rim. The crossing points on the spokes will be tied together with thin wire and soldered to further increase rigidity. The chain and sprocket wheels are wider than those on a road bike, and this creates a stiffer transmission.

Before the advent of ski-binding type fixings with which racing cyclists clip their shoes to the pedals, some track riders, who need to absolutely at one with their machine, used to bolt their shoes to the pedals, lacing themselves in for a race while a helper held them upright.

(Left) To go, stop. Cat and mouse as the front sprinter stops on the banking, trying to force his opponent to take the lead.

(Below) A competitor's view of the USSR Olympic and World Champion sprinter Kvosh. In this race Kvosh has yet to make his move.

(Top) The USSR is a strong nation in sprinting and pursuiting. This is their 4000 metre pursuit champion, Ekimov, flat out.

(Above) Tony Doyle, Individual Pro Pursuit Champion, was nearly killed in a crash during a Six-day race in Munich in 1989.

(Right) Team pursuiting. Only three riders out of the team of four are actually required to finish the race.

Pursuiting

Pursuiting is the antithesis of sprinting: minimal tactics are involved and the race is run at a constant speed, like a TT. The two riders start simultaneously at opposite sides of the track and literally pursue each other. The men's amateur and pro events are over four and five km respectively, and the women's over three. Pedalling technique is all important, since every drop of energy must be turned into forward motion (and not into rocking the bike from side to side, for

example). As each rider completes a lap, a light flashes so that spectators can see who is leading.

The modern pursuiting bike, which has evolved enormously in the last five years, is as different from the sprint machine as the two races are from each other. In 1989, the twenty year old British rider Colin Sturgess won the World Pro Pursuit Championship on a low profile frame made from Italian Columbus SLX tubing by British frame builder Harry Quinn. It had curved top and seat tubes, giving an ultrashort wheelbase. Although SLX tubing builds into a very stiff frame, the three main-tube joints were reinforced with triangular inserts of sheet steel, and the forks built with aerodynamic teardrop shaped tubing. The bike had a rear disc wheel with the choice of a disc or 28 spoked front wheel (Sturgess used the disc). The rear wheel was shod with a slick-treaded six ounce (150 gram) tubular tyre inflated to around 160 psi.

Team pursuit

The team pursuit is like a high precision version of the team TT in a road race. Four-man teams pursue each other over 3.1 miles (5 km) with each rider taking a half-lap turn on the front. Riders will be all in the same gear, pedalling in unison and riding much closer to each other than they would in a road race. In the 1989 Worlds the East Germans took first place in the 4 min 16.58 sec. The much higher pace that a team can sustain is highlighted by comparing the team time with Sturgess's individual time of 5 min 52.40 sec.

The formidable Czech team pursuit in action. Soviet and Eastern Europe riders tend to use western manufactured equipment. Note the inverted handle-bars, disc wheels, aerodynamic helmets and lycra clothing.

Kilometer time-trial

In the individual kilometer TT the rider covers just three laps of the track. As soon as the starting gun goes, he must crank up his gear as quickly as possible and pour all his effort into the brief ride. The 1989 World title was won by Jens Glucklich of East Germany in a remarkable 1 min 4.032 sec.

Points race

The points race is a distance event for perhaps 24 riders. In a race of 90 or 100 laps there will be a sprint every five, for which points are awarded. Breaks form just as in a road race, and they will try to build up a lap lead on the bunch to secure victory. Points races are fast and furious, despite the distance, and with so many riders crashes are not uncommon.

Motor-paced race

In motor-paced racing each rider 'sits in' behind a special pacing motorbike equipped with a powerful engine capable of driving big gears so that a constant speed can be maintained. The driver of the motorbike – 'the pacer' – sits bolt upright to act as a windbreak for the 'stayer'. The pacer really controls the race tactics, while the stayer simply endeavours to keep in contact.

The motorbike has a roller positioned across the back to prevent a crash if the stayer accidentally touches with his front wheel. To allow him to get as close as possible to the pacer, the stayer rides on a strange bike with a small front wheel sitting in reversed forks. The bike has a

reinforcing bar between the fork crown and the handlebars to help the rider control the steering as he goes round the banking at a speed of 40 mph (64 kph).

Despite the presence on the track of eight pairs of machines, quite a lot of manoeuvring goes on in a race, and the noise and speed make it a thrilling, if strange, spectacle. The 1989 winners of the hour-long pro race was Giovanni Renosto and pacer Walter Carradin of Italy, while the winners of the 31.2 mile (50 km) amateur event were Roland Konigshofer and Karl Igl

The unusual motor-paced race has eight pairs of bikes on the track and the speed, noise and manoeuvring make an exciting blend. Riders shout instructions to the pacer.

of Austria in 42 hr 30 min 19 sec. Unlike pursuiting bikes, motor-paced cycles have changed little over the years: Konigshofer suffered no disadvantages in riding a 21 year old machine.

Keirin

The Keirin, a professional-only event, is similar to motor-paced racing except that the pacers swing off the track with one lap to go and the riders sprint unpaced to the finish. Riders jostle to get into a favourable position from which to launch the final lap attack, and usually a team-mate will lead-out a fellow sprinter before peeling off with 200 metres to go. In the 1989 Championships Vincenzo Ceci paced his team mate Claudio Golinelli to victory in this fashion.

Besides these various events there is one other record distance which deserves mention: the hour unpaced record on the track. This is a one hour individual TT in which the rider amasses as many kilometres as possible. The record holder is Francesco Moser, who broke Eddy Merckx's 1972 record in 1984. Moser actually made two rides, the first at high altitude in Mexico City, where the thin air gave him a 0.85 mile (1.25 km) advantage over his subsequent sea level record which was set two years later in Milan. Moser clocked 51.15135 km in Mexico, and 49.80193 km in Milan.

Although Moser's records were celebrated, the manner in which he achieved them was heavily criticised. No-one could complain about the scientific way he trained for the Mexico attempt, using an array of medical technology to monitor his fitness levels, but his use of blood doping was condemned. The controversy was compounded by Moser's use of a low profile machine, fitted with disc wheels which were specially weighted to increase their flywheel

(Above) The great Italian Francesco Moser, four times holder of the world hour record. (Right) With one lap to go in the motor-paced Keirin, the motor bike swings off the track and leaves the riders sprint to the finish.

effect, before the use of such equipment had been officially sanctioned. Moser subsequently compounded the controversy when he rode a bike with an oversized backwheel which served to increase the flywheel effect even more.

Six-day racing. Early events in the USA caused public protests.

Six-day racing

Six-day racing, like greyhound racing and wrestling, is as much a form of 'entertainment' as it is a sport, and takes place in European indoor velodromes in the winter months. Racing begins at about 4 pm and continues into the early hours of the morning.

As its name suggests, the event lasts six days, and the mainstay of a six is the 'Madison' which takes its name from the Madison Square Gardens velodrome where it was invented. In the American track scene of the 1890s, endurance races were popular attractions in which riders had to lap for up to 24 hours without sleep. But the harrowing scenes that resulted from these enforced periods on the bike eventually turned public opinion against it and in 1899, time restrictions were placed on racing and then two-man relay teams were introduced at Madison Square Gardens.

Six-day racing declined in the USA in 1929, and the last six to be held in Britain was at Wembley arena in 1981, but racing is thriving in Europe with about fifteen meetings every year in cities like Ghent, Zurich, Paris, Rotterdam, Copenhagen, Grenoble and Munich.

Approximately 12 teams will compete in a Madison. While half the field ride round at 30 mph (48 kph), sprinting for points every ten laps, the other half will coast around the outer edge of the track. When a rider tires, he will 'hand sling' his partner into the race by grabbing his hand and launching him away. In other respects the Madison is like the points race described above.

In order to introduce variety into the long programme, the Madisons will be interspersed with

(Opposite) A Six-day event in Rotterdam. Inside the track there is usually a dining area, live music and basic team facilities. Masseurs keep riders in shape as Madisons can last for up to two hours. Crowds for these events can range from 7,000 to 20,000.

(Left) The 'Hand sling'. A tired rider launches a teammate into the race during a Madison. These events can be dangerous as riders are travelling at high speed in comparatively limited space. Crashes, when they happen, can be serious.

perhaps a tandem sprint, a motor paced race or a Derny race, which is a variation on motor paced racing using a much smaller motorcycles called Dernys. In the 'Devil' – devil take the hindmost – the last rider in the bunch to complete each lap drops out until only the winner remains.

Even though six-day racing is a lot easier than it was a hundred years ago it is still very hard work, with long hours spent in a hot, harsh and high-pressured atmosphere. There is usually a dining area inside the track where spectators eat, drink and fill the air with cigarette smoke, while a jazz or rock band at one end of the circuit pumps out loud music all night.

Two remarkable riders who have enjoyed a particularly successful Madison partnership are Tasmanian Danny Clark, and the British rider Tony Doyle, who as well as riding a full season

A Derny race with Holland's Zoetemelk and France's Fignon. Top riders can earn very well indeed from these races and also keep fit during the winter.

of Sixes is also a succesful pro with the British Ever Ready road team. Doyle has won 21 Sixes since 1980, 18 of them with Clark. They are so invincible as a team that organizers periodically pair them with a different partner to vary the competition. At the Cologne Six in 1989, Doyle was paired with the veteran roadman Dietrich Thureau, who won fifteen stages of the 1977 Tour de France. But Thureau crashed and collided with two Dernys, breaking his ankle, while Clark's partner Volker Diehl retired with a trapped nerve in his back, and so the reunited Clark and Doyle went on to win.

Cycle speedway

One little known track sport that is enjoying a rapid resurgence of interest is Cycle Speedway. Races take four laps of a tight, flat, dirt covered circuit, about 90 metres round. Races are rough and fast, lasting little longer than 45 seconds. The season runs from April to September. The bikes are similar to track bikes except that they have upturned handlebars, a single speed freewheel and knobbly tyres. There is more physical contact than in any other branch of cycle sport and riders frequently take tumbles. The racing is now attracting big money from Coca-Cola and the UK Daily Mirror newspaper, which sponsor the National Championship.

Cycle speedway. The British National Championships at Thurrock, 1989. Spills are common. Newspaper sponsorship has helped to promote this sport.

Cyclo-cross

Cyclo-cross is a winter sport and, as its name suggests, is something like moto-cross on bicycles. It began early in the century and World Championships were first held in the 1920s. The course is usually a circuit consisting of metalled road, muddy tracks and steep banks on which, at various points, obstacles such as logs or ditches have to be negotiated. A typical circuit will be a mile or so round, and a race will cover twelve laps and last about a hour. The race is a demanding test both of a rider's fitness and his bike-handling skills, and the nature of the course is such that riders are obliged to dismount and run with their bikes at certain points.

A cyclo-cross bike is built with a longer wheelbase than a road bike, to improve stability and handling on steep descents and slippery corners. Like most mountain-bikes it has cantilever brakes which have far greater stopping power than calipers, and gear levers on the handlebar ends. The wheels are shod with knobbly tyres. Many riders have two or more such machines, and while they ride one, a helper will clean the other. At a convenient point on the course the bikes will be exchanged, sometimes as often as every lap, depending on conditions.

While 'cross is highly demanding in terms of stamina and skill, tactics are minimal. As soon as a race starts, riders will jostle for front position, and whoever is lucky enough to get there often stays in place: because the course is treacherous and often narrow, overtaking is very difficult.

Steve Douce, a British pro who rides on the road in the summer, is also a succesful 'cross-

rider. While many pros want a break from riding in the winter, Douce sees 'cross as an excellent way of keeping fit and preparing for the summer season. In 1989 he won his sixth National Championship, covering 12 miles (9.5 km) in 1 hr 9 min 49 sec. There is a saying that 'racing is the best form of training', and given their successes on the road, this would certainly seem to hold true for Tony Doyle and Steve Douce.

Cyclo-cross. British Junior International Roger Hammond tackles a hill carrying his bike. A typical circuit race will be over about 10 miles and last about an hour.

(Above) Steve Douce, who rides on the road during the summer and who is a successful 'cross rider during the winter.

(Left) Cyclo-cross. Young riders keep the momentum going up a steep climb. Most riders have two machines and a helper will provide a clean one as often as every lap.

Mountain-bike racing

Mountain-biking started in California in the late 1970s, and the first bikes started arriving in Britain in the early '80s. Despite their high cost, trade in the machines has soared, accounting for between fifty and seventy-five percent of all cycle sales in Britain and the USA.

For some people a mountain-bike is a chic accessory like a Mont Blanc pen or a Filofax; for many more it is the ideal commuting bike, robust, stable and visible. But an increasing number are used off-road on forest tracks, bridle paths and disused railway lines, which is what they were designed for. The mountain-bike has a long wheelbase, some eighteen medium to low gears, cantilever brakes, wide tyres and flat handlebars with all controls within reach of the fingertips when both hands are on the bars.

Mountain-bike racing (and the sponsorship to encourage it) has developed very rapidly in the 1980s, especially in the USA, where there are a number of pro teams. There are busy calendars of regional, national and international events. Although similar to cyclo-cross, races tend to be over harder, more extreme terrain, with the emphasis on climbing and descending, so much so that some races consist of a single descent of a mountain. One such race is the 'Repack Downhill', held in Marin County, California, which descends 1300 feet (430 m) in 1.8 miles (2.9 km), with riders reaching speeds of up to 30 mph (48 kph).

As well as attracting all kinds of amateur enthusiasts, top professional cyclo-cross riders

like Peugeot squad riders David Baker and Tim Gould and American pro World Champion Mike Kloser participate in events like the Grundig World Cup series, where each round offers a purse of some £47,000. Perhaps the most unusual race in the British calendar is the Man versus Horse marathon, which is run over 22 miles (37 km) in the Welsh mountains, with 4000 feet (1330 m) of climbing. The race is a three way competition between mountain bikes, runners and horse riders.

Mountain-biking is still in its infancy; and

Mountain-bike racing is now taking off in a big way in Great Britain and the USA.

when racing first began, cycling clubs and cyclo-cross organizations took a rather negative view of developments. But they have mostly come round to the idea now, and given the growing popularity of off-road riding, and the increasingly crowded and dangerous state of the roads, it is surely set to become a major branch of cycle sport.

(Left) Mountain-bikers climb a steep ascent
at Parc Cwm Darran, mid-Glamorgan.
(Top) Terrain is often tougher than
that used for cyclo-cross.

Time-trialling

Time-trialling in Europe: The 'race of truth'

We have seen how important the time-trial can be in a stage race like the Tour de France, where in 1989 three of the 21 stages were individual TTs. In Europe the TT is known as the 'race of truth' and it is easy to see why. The rider is out on his own, with no-one to pace him, no-one to shelter behind in a head wind and no team-mates to block for him while he makes good his escape. Everything is down to him.

Although the individual TT is recognized as an important test of a rider's skill and courage, in Europe it is not practised as a sport in its own right, as in Britain. In Europe there are just two important TTs for professional riders: the Grand Prix des Nations and the Trofeo Baracchi for two-man teams. The Baracchi course, which covers 60.3 miles (96.6 km) of Italian road was completed by the 1989 winners Laurent Fignon and Thierry Marie in a time of 1 hr 54 min 48 sec, an average speed of 31.6 mph (50.5 kph).

In a 'two-up' team time-trial each rider takes it in turn to ride flat out in front for perhaps 200 metres at a time, before dropping back to shelter behind the other rider. Once in the front man's slipstream, the back rider can ease up and get out of oxygen debt before going to the front again. In this way the pair can keep a much higher pace than one rider could on his own, but they must have a good rapport, and be well drilled in the procedure of coming off the front and tucking in behind without falling back too far. If the rider behind slips back, he will fall out of the slipstream and need to sprint to recover,

wasting valuable energy. In order to get the maximum benefit from the slipstream the rider behind must ride as close as he dares to the front man's back wheel, which requires great concentration, courage and a rock steady pace.

Two weeks after his Baracchi win, Fignon won again in the Individual Grand Prix des Nations. In this race, riders complete two laps of a 27.9 miles (44.5 km) circuit which begins and ends on the sea front at Cannes. With its steep climbs, and treacherous descents, the course is as much a test of a rider's bike-handling skill as it is of his ability to ride unpaced against the clock. Fignon set a new course record of 1 hr 56 min 57 sec for the 56 miles (89 km), a remarkable ride in view of the strong headwind over the last 2.5 miles (4 km).

Time-trialling in Britain

In Britain, time-trialling is a popular sport in its own right, with its own governing body, the Road Time Trials Council (RTTC). There is a simple explanation for this. Racing on the road had been banned in 1889 and even inconspicuous TTs held on quiet lanes were often interrupted by the police. Furthermore, once a rider was under way he had to take care not to be seen 'riding furiously' as the law termed it. In order to avoid detection, riders wore black tights and jackets. Race details, posted to competitors before the event, were marked 'confidential' and courses were denoted by a secret code, a practice that persists to this day.

In 1922 the Road Racing Council was formed, and was renamed the RTTC in 1937. In 1930 the season-long British Best All-rounder (BBAR) competition was inaugurated. The winner is the competitor with the highest average speed taken from three qualifying rides over distances of 50 and 100 miles (80 and 160 km), and a 12 hour ride, in which a great a distance as possible is amassed. A similar competition for women is held at 25, 50 and 100 miles.

In addition to the fixed distances of the BAR competition, there are numerous events at 10 miles (16 km) which, along with 25 miles (40 km), is by far the most popular distance, with dozens of events every weekend, as well as mid-week evening races in the summer. A new 10 mile record of 18 min 48 sec was set in 1988 by Colin Sturgess, who is now a pro with the Belgian ADR team, and who won the World Pro Pursuit Championship on the track in 1989.

The TT season starts in late February. In past years the early season was a time for 'restricted gear' or 'medium gear' events, which were usually ridden on a fixed wheel cycle with a maximum gearing of 72 inches. In order to complete 25 miles (40 km) in 56 min 30 sec Tony Doyle had to pedal at 124 rpm in the Crabwood CC race held in February 1980. Early season medium gear events have declined in popularity in recent years, and many riders now prefer to ride two-up or three-up Team TTs or hilly races over shortish distances ranging from 11 to 26 miles (18 to 42 km).

(Above) Colin Sturgess, who was World Pro Pursuit Champion in 1989 and who holds the 10 miles (16km) record.

(Right) Tony Doyle, who completed 25 miles (40 km) in 56 min 30 sec in the Crabwood CC TT in February 1980.

(Above) Baker Alf Engers, whose 25 mile (40km) record has stood for twenty years. Note that he set this record on an ordinary road bike.

(Left) The TT season starts in late February. This means that training can take place in difficult weather conditions, here in snow.

As the season progresses these give way to the fixed distance events, with the longer distance rides being held in mid-summer. In contrast to Colin Sturgess's 10 mile (16 km) record, the 25 mile (40 km) record has stood for twenty years. It was set by a baker, Alf Engers, whose time of 49 min 24 sec (30.04 mph/48.06 kph) was achieved in 1969 on a course which uses a stretch of dual carriageway (two-lane) road between Chelmsford and Colchester in Essex. Engers set the record on an ordinary road bike with spoked wheels and normal handlebars with exposed brake cables.

Aerodynamics and technological developments

Although there is no doubt that aerodynamic disc wheels could give an advantage of up to two minutes over a distance of 25 miles (40 km), this has to be weighed against the handling problems that riders experience with discs in a cross wind. Furthermore, disc wheels are a lot heavier than spoked. On a flat course (ideally on a track) the extra weight creates a flywheel effect which is clearly advantageous. But as soon as they have to be ridden uphill, that weight turns into a disadvantage, just as weight is a disadvantage for heavy riders in the mountain stages of the Tour de France.

Time savings can be made costing little or nothing compared to the price of an expensive disc wheel. It is the rider's body, not the bicycle, which offers the greatest resistance to the wind, and time can be saved over 25 miles (40 km) by

discarding loose, flapping clothing and donning a one-piece lycra skin-suit, as worn by downhill skiers and 100 metre sprinters. Further time can be saved by crouching as low as possible on the bike while maintaining a flat back, and more can be trimmed away simply by pulling one's elbows in.

It follows that the recent fashion for low profile bicycles has not significantly reduced riders' times, except perhaps on the track where the difference between an Olympic gold and silver is measured in a few hundredths of a second. Compared to the profile of the competitor's body, such refinements as a sloping top-tube, teardrop or oval section frame tubing and concealed cables make only a tiny difference. The main advantage of the low profile bike, besides the psychological one, is that it encourages the rider himself to adopt a low profile riding position.

The quest for speed

Because time-trialling in Britain has been concerned primarily with record breaking rather than winning races, there is an obsession with pure speed – with improving one's time – that is absent from the TT stages of a road race. Top

Lycra material, also worn by skiers, helps riders reduce their body resistance to the wind. The rider is John Pritchard.

riders will travel very long distances to compete on 'superfast' courses, which means, in practice, flat, well-surfaced dual carriageway (US: divided highway). Most time-trial courses are 'out and back' along the same stretch of road, so that, in a 25 mile (40 km) trial for example, any advantage enjoyed on the outward half, such as a tailwind or downward slope, is cancelled out on the return leg. Yet it is a curious fact that 14 miles (22 km) of tailwind might be needed to balance the effect of 11 miles (18 km) of headwind. Hence riders take weather conditions extremely seriously: the ideal day will be cool and calm, with low air pressure.

In addition to being flat and well surfaced, the superfast courses usually carry a fairly high volume of traffic and it is well known to all cyclists that passing vehicles create a suction effect, allowing the rider to accelerate for a few valuable seconds.

The obsessive preoccupation with achieving a conjunction of peak fitness, the right equipment and course on a good day has distorted the sport (although it has led to some very fast

(Far left) The legendary Beryl Burton who broke not only the women's but also the men's 12 hours distance record. None of her other records have been broken.

(Left) TT specialist Ian Cammish is grateful for a refreshing sponge. Cammish excels at the 50 and 100 miles TTs.

times). The joyless pursuit of speed and the ever-increasing volumes of traffic on main roads has led to the growing popularity of TTs on hilly or 'sporting' courses, similar to that used for the Grand Prix des Nations. Most time-triallists agree that this is where the future lies: some of the fastest courses have already been banned on safety grounds, a trend likely to continue.

Beryl Burton and Ian Cammish

Post war time-trialling in Britain has been dominated by two legendary figures: Beryl Burton and Ian Cammish. Beryl Burton has excelled at all distances and has won more competitions than any other cyclist, man or woman. She set new women's 10 mile (16 km) records every year from 1960 to 1973, except 1966, with the 1973 record standing at 21 min 25 sec. At 25 miles (40 km) she did likewise from 1959 to 1976, recording a final time of 53 min 21 sec. Over the same period she improved the 50 miles (80 km) record from 2 hr 6 min 38 sec to 1 hr 51min 30 sec. At 100 miles (160 km) she set records from 1958 to 1968, culminating in a time of 3 hr 55 min 05 sec, an average speed of 25.1 mph (40.1 kph).

Perhaps her greatest achievement was her 1967 12 hour distance of 277.25 miles (443.6 km) in which she broke not only the women's record but the men's too. None of Burton's records has yet been broken and it is quite possible that, as road racing continues to increase in popularity while time-trialling declines, they never will be.

A rider shows signs of strain during the 24 hours TT. Many riders retire in the early morning. Those who survive till dawn usually finish.

Latterly, Ian Cammish has more or less put the men's 50 and 100 mile (80 and 160 km) records out of reach. Cammish has made little impression on the distances either side, preferring to excel at 100 miles (160 km). He has achieved no less than 28 rides under four hours, and in 1983 set a staggering time of 3 hr, 31 min 53 sec, an average speed of 28.2 mph (45.1

At the far end of the distance scale, in the midst of the mid-summer cluster of 12 hour events, comes the 24 hours, one of the oldest established on the calendar. For many years this was a popular fixture, but interest has dwindled to the point where there are only two left. In the National Championship, which in 1989 was held in Cheshire, the first rider sets off at 2 pm. The field ride through the afternoon until night falls. At dusk lights are fitted and warm clothes put on, and the race moves onto a well-lit circuit. Many riders retire in the early hours of the morning, victims of exhaustion and the monotony of riding round the night loop. At dawn the race moves onto a new set of roads, and those who get this far usually finish. The record distance of 507 miles (811 km) was set by Roy Cromack in 1969.

Excited spectators cheer on a rider as he nears the end of an exhausting hill climb. These events attract road racers, more than time-triallists.

Technique

The essential qualities of good time-trialling besides fitness, are courage, judgement and concentration. A rider must get into a smooth pedalling rhythm as quickly as possible and once this has been established, absolute concentration is required to maintain it, especially on a hilly course or over a long distance. The time-triallist has to judge his effort as accurately as possible, ideally arriving at the line with no energy to spare. To really reach this point, he will have to push himself, sometimes through the pain barrier, and this takes courage.

Hill climbs

The end of the season in October is heralded by a month or so of hill climbs, which are, quite simply, uphill time-trials. Hills are generally short and steep, consisting of perhaps 1500 metres of one in seven gradient. These events often attract road racers rather than time-triallists, who tend to be frightened of hills. Riders who make a speciality of hill climbing will ride as light a bike as possible, with a single gear fixed wheel, ultra-light rims and one front brake. When Malcolm Elliott, now a pro with the Spanish Teka team, won the National Championship in 1980, he even had aluminium bearings in his steering column in order to save weight, and the 1988 winner, Chris Boardman, shed fourteen pounds as part of his preparation. Although a pure climbing event, the National Championships have recently been won, not by pure climbers, but talented all-rounders.

Record breaking

Besides the out and back TT, there are numerous 'straight out' records, as well as various place to place records such as Lands End to John O'Groats in Britain and the RAAM – Race across America. The record for Lands End to John O'-Groats, 870 miles (1390 km) from the south-west tip of Cornwall to the north-eastern corner of mainland Scotland was set by John Wood-burn in 1982. Woodburn covered the distance in 45 hr 3 min 16 sec. The RAAM, from Hunt-ington Beach, California to Atlantic City, New Jersey, covers a distance of 3107 miles (5000 km). The current men's record is held by Pete Penseyres with 8 days 9 hr and 47 min and the women's record of 10 days 2 hr and 4 min is held by Elaine Mariolle. In 1986 a one-legged Briton, Hugh Culverhouse completed the dis-tance in 13 days, 11 hr and 1 min.

Besides these events, there have been speed record attempts since the earliest days of cycling. Perhaps the most famous of these was in 1899, by the American Charles Murphy, who was known as 'Mile-a-minute Murphy'. He rode behind a steam locomotive on a special wooden track laid between a 2.5 mile (4 km) stretch of line at Hampstead Plains, Long Island. At the first attempt the loco was unable to achieve the required speed of 60 mph (96 kmh) and a bigger one was brought in. At the eighth attempt

Dick Poole receives welcome encouragement during an attempt on Lands End to John O'Groats record. Current record is just over 45 hours.

(Opposite, far left) Dick Poole. (Opposite) Jill Clapton.
(Above) A recumbent cycle or HPV.

The Triathlon consists of a swim, a bike-ride and run in that order.
Here is the start of the race as competitors start the swim.

Murphy managed to ride for one mile behind the train in 57.9 seconds, pedalling in a cloud of dust and clad only in black tights and a long sleeved jersey. The current World speed record of 152.284 mph (243.654 kmh) is held by the American John Howard. It was set on Bonneville salt flats, Utah, in 1985. Howard rode behind a specially modified racing car.

Human powered vehicles

Another fringe activity in which sophisticated know-how is applied to the humble bicycle in pursuit of speed is HPV racing. The HPV is basically a recumbent cycle on which the rider lies rather than sits, and the whole is enclosed within a rigid aerodynamic skin. The advantage that this arrangement gives has resulted in some

remarkable achievements. In 1988 one such machine reached 65 mph (104 kmh) at the du Pont prize meeting in Colorado.

The majority of HPVs are home-made by enthusiasts. But there is also a 'big-money', hi-tec end to the scene. The most thrilling departure in this area has been the Daedalus light aircraft project, which is backed by the Smithsonian Institute, MIT and the brewers Michelob. The human powered plane is made from graphite-epoxy resin and carbon fibre, and even with its wingspan of over 100 feet (30 m), weighs only 70 pounds. Tests were carried out at NASA flight laboratories in California and in 1988 the prototype 'Light Eagle' successfully flew from Heraklion on mainland Greece, to the island of Santorini, a distance of 74 miles.

Triathlon

The sport of triathlon has grown very fast since it was first conceived in the early '70s. The triathlon consists of a swim, a bike ride and a run, usually in that order. Triathlons are held over four distances, with the 'sprint' comprising a 1000 metre swim, 20 mile bike ride and 10 km run. At the other extreme the 'Ironman' involves a 3.8 km swim, 112 mile bike ride and 42.2 km (marathon) run.

For people attracted to cycling but who want to exercise their upper body as well, triathlons are an attractive alternative to plain cycling. But in order to succeed, participants have to develop a busy and complex training schedule, and it is a fact that virtually all the top triathletes train and race fulltime.

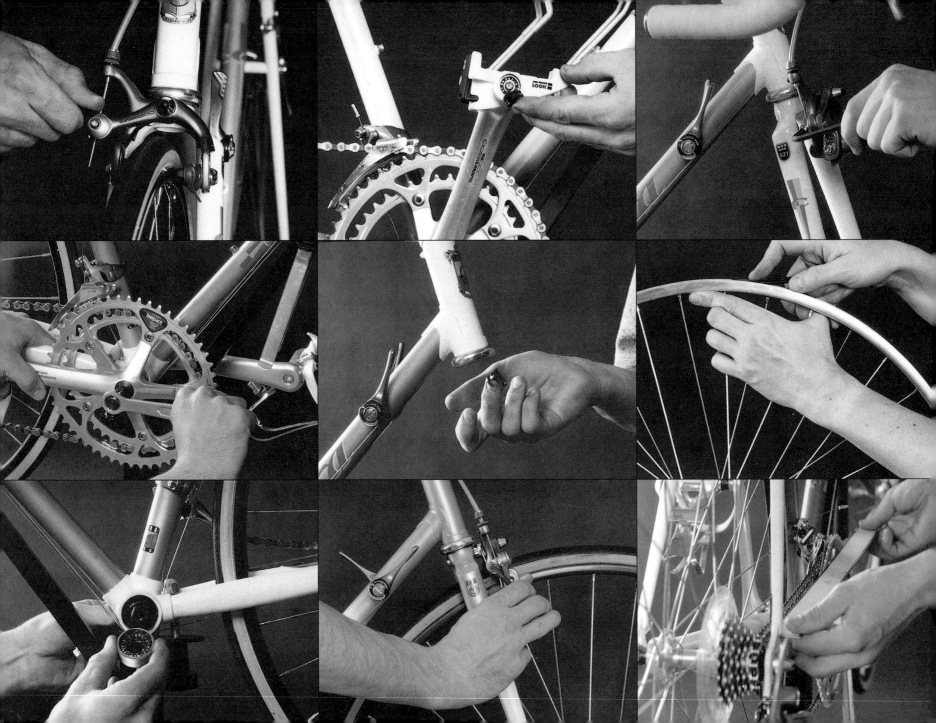

Repair and maintenance

Cleaning

Every bike should be a clean bike, and if it is not, then it should be. It is impossible to effectively maintain any machine unless it is clean. You can not diagnose faults easily, or check components. If a bike is covered in dirt, then it will work its way into the bearings.

Modern materials have made cleaning a bike much easier. Paint finishes are much harder and frames are often stove enameled and/or chromed. Components too are now almost universally made from anodized alloy, which means that they can resist salt and grime and can be wiped clean.

It depends on how dirty your bike is as to which cleaning methods you need to resort to. In the summer usually little more than a damp cloth is needed to wipe away the dust and then a soft dry cloth to bring everything up shining and new.

Even in the summer there will be a build-up of grime on the chainring teeth and on the free-wheel sprockets if you have been overly generous with the lubricant spray. A de-greasing spray, as recommended in the lubrication section, is the most useful for destroying this grime. Remove the chain from the chainrings and spray either side of the chainset on to the teeth, then wipe off the dirt. To clean the sprockets remove the rear wheel, but take great care not to get any of the spray into the hub bearings, or into the freewheel mechanism. Spray down-

wards on to the freewheel sprockets and then again wipe off the muck.

White spirit applied with a soft cloth can also be used for removing smaller quantities of grime built up in these areas.

Very dirty bikes, including mud encrusted mountain bikes are best cleaned with a high pressure hose. First blast the mud off, then spray a multi-purpose car cleaner with a de-greaser on to the frame and components before rinsing off. A soft brush is handy to help remove muck from hard-to-reach areas around the bottom bracket and the fork ends.

It is important not to spray the water or the cleaning spray directly into the bearings. Once a bike has been cleaned with a hose, it should be dried either with a soft cloth or a chamois leather and then the chain should be lubricated.

Although the complete bicycle may not always need cleaning this thoroughly, the wheels and especially the rims will collect considerable muck from the road and the de-greasing spray will be needed to clean this.

After spraying the affected area, all dirt and surplus spray will need to be wiped away and then the rim, spokes and hubs can be buffed up with a soft cloth.

Never put any polish on the rims as this will reduce braking efficiency and will usually result in the brakes making loud squealing noises.

Spend time cleaning the spokes as eventually

these may show signs of rust, but the application of a small amount of lubricant spray should solve this problem.

You should also inspect the brake blocks for any tiny stones when cleaning the bike. These should be removed with a small screwdriver to prevent them from damaging the rim and reducing braking efficiency. If brake blocks are too worn, or damaged, replace them.

Don't forget the tyres(US:tires). When cleaning, check the treads for cuts, removing any flints which may have become lodged. If a tyre is too badly damaged it should be replaced.

The side walls of the tyre should be wiped clean, but solvents should not be used, especially with tubulars which have very delicate side walls.

Strong metal polishes should not be used for cleaning the alloy surfaces as these can damage the anodized finish. After washing down it should be possible to polish with a soft cloth.

Although cycle components do not often crack or fracture it is during cleaning that you will spot the danger signs. Pay special attention to the cranks where they join the bottom bracket axle and around the pedal thread. Also check the frame around the lugs and any brazed-on fittings, plus the handlebars, stem, seat pillar and pedal plates.

Don't forget the brake and gear cables. Any frayed cables should be replaced at once.

1 Brushing dirt from the hub flanges

2 Cleaning freewheel with solvent and brush

3 Sponging dirt from handlebar tape

4 Cleaning the brake mechanism

5 Brushing the chain

6 Wiping excess lubricant from the chain

7 Spraying the chain with lubricant

8 Brushing off excess lubricant

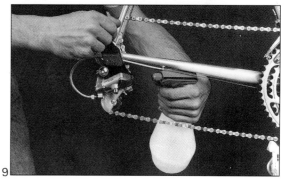

9 Lubricating the rear gear mechanism

Lubrication

Cycle lubrication is now a sophisticated subject and is more involved than a can of household oil and a tin of sticky grease. The idea is not to simply stop components from going rusty, but to provide the best possible operating conditions for the chain and bearings.

The first thing you will need to buy is a can of spray lubricant, but don't worry, almost all of these sprays are now ozone friendly. They are a basic requirement of the chain and will need applying at least once a month.

Remember when spraying the chain that the area which needs the lubrication is the centre. You need to oil the tiny rollers on which the chain pivots, not the outer plates of the chain.

Many chains today are chrome-plated and do not rust easily, but even if you have a standard black chain the best way to lubricate the whole chain is to place a piece of rag under it and then spray the lubricant down into the rollers. It is easiest to work on the upper section of chain between the freewheel and the chainset. Do not spray the lubricant into the freewheel or chainset area; it is not normally needed on these components.

Rotate the pedals backwards to gradually spray each section of the chain. Keep the rag in position until after you have finished, then by gripping it around the chain and winding the pedals backwards, you will wipe the excess lubricant around the outside of the chain plates, cleaning them and when the oil evaporates, leaving a clear protective coating.

The other advantage of cleaning a chain in

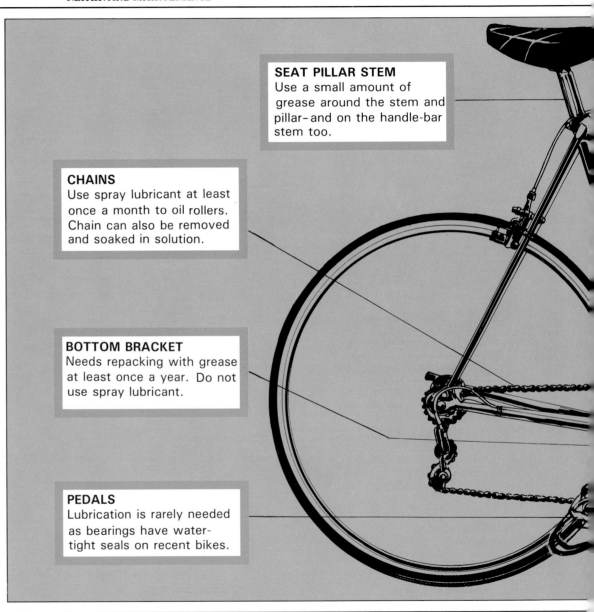

SEAT PILLAR STEM
Use a small amount of grease around the stem and pillar – and on the handle-bar stem too.

CHAINS
Use spray lubricant at least once a month to oil rollers. Chain can also be removed and soaked in solution.

BOTTOM BRACKET
Needs repacking with grease at least once a year. Do not use spray lubricant.

PEDALS
Lubrication is rarely needed as bearings have water-tight seals on recent bikes.

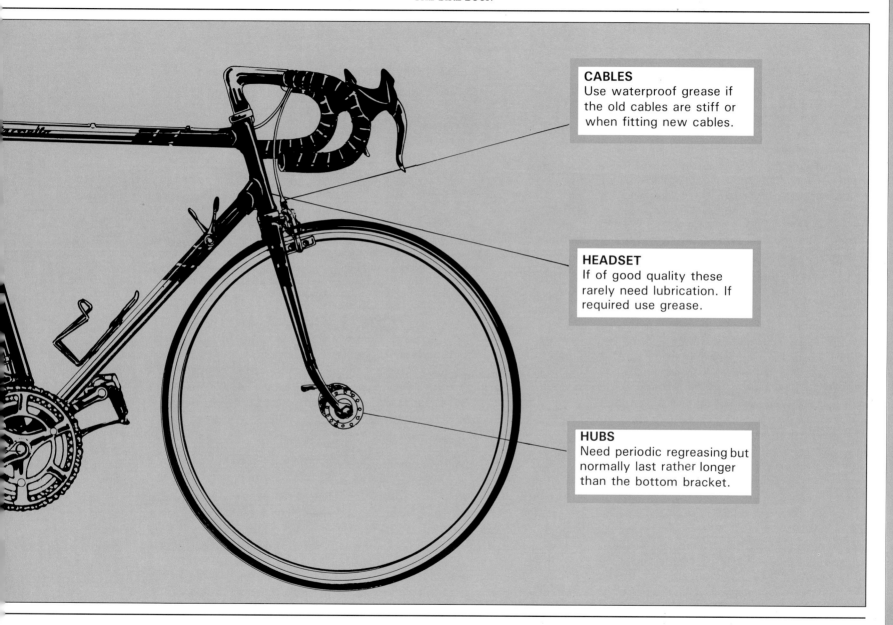

CABLES
Use waterproof grease if the old cables are stiff or when fitting new cables.

HEADSET
If of good quality these rarely need lubrication. If required use grease.

HUBS
Need periodic regreasing but normally last rather longer than the bottom bracket.

LUBRICATION

this way is that it avoids getting the lubricant in unwanted areas such as onto the rim of the back wheel. A build-up of evaporated lubricant in this area reduces braking efficiently.

How often the chain needs lubricating depends on the amount of use and the operating conditions. A mountain bike ridden in muddy winter conditions will need a liberal application of lubricant after the machine has been washed.

In the summer, dust and grit are the enemies, but it would be unusual to have to lubricate the chain more than once a week.

Lubricant sprays will drive out water and grit and so when used in more liberal quantities can be used to clean a chain. Always wipe surface dirt such as mud away before you apply the spray.

Once a chain has been used for a prolonged period, or in very bad conditions, it will work better if it is cleaned. It is not necessary to remove the chain from the bike if you use a de-greasing spray. This will remove all the grime if it is sprayed in to the chain in the same way that the lubricant was applied with a rag to catch any excess, which is then wiped around the outer plates. Several applications using a clean rag each time will get the best results. Various types of suitable spray are sold in cycle or motor accessory shops. Although such sprays are relatively new to the cycle trade they have been used for some time on motorcycles and cars where the grease and grime build-up is substantially increased.

Other chain cleaners require the chain to be

Replacing gear cables. For full, step by step detail concerning gear servicing and replacement, see pages 149-151.

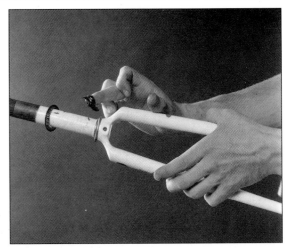

Packing grease around the fork column race of the headset. For full details of headset servicing see page 143.

removed and placed in a container where it can be soaked in a cleaning solution. Although this method is more thorough, it is more time consuming and perhaps too extensive for most riders' needs. If a chain becomes too dirty and clogged it can always be replaced. With a normal amount of riding a new chain will be necessary every year.

In wet winter conditions when there is a lot of grime and grit on the roads, it will be an advantage to spray a limited amount of the lubricant on to the freewheel sprockets. The pedals should be rotated backwards so as to turn the freewheel and an equal amount of spray will be distributed over the cluster to drive out water and dirt. Do not use too much as just a limited amount will evaporate to leave a protective film

which will aid rapid gear changes.

It may sometimes be necessary to spray other moving mechanical parts on the bicycle should they become sticky. A little lubrication on joints of the rear gear mechanism or the front gear changer will often improve performance as would a sparing amount of lubricant sprayed on to the springs and pivot of the brake stirrups.

Spray lubricant should not be used for the bearing areas of the bike such as the bottom bracket, hubs or the headset.

All bearings are packed in grease and the lubricant spray will only dilute the grease, making it thinner and less efficient. Only in an emergency, say with a squeaky pedal, should the lubricant spray be used, but this is only a short-term solution as the pedal will eventually

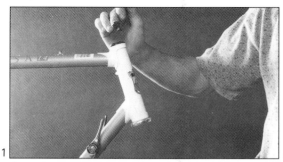

1 Greasing the top race of the headset. For full details of headset servicing see page 143.

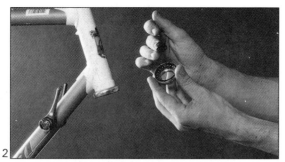

2 The headset's bearing cage placed in the adjusting race and smeared with grease. See page 143.

3 Bottom bracket servicing. Full step by step details can be found on page 144.

4 Freewheel cassette greasing. Step by step details can be found on page 145.

5 Pedal bearing servicing. The complete sequence can be followed on page 145.

need stripping down and repacking with grease.

A high quality, thin waterproof grease should be used. Although this is more expensive, it will last longer and so will save having to strip components down too frequently.

Old-fashioned conventional grease has the consistency and the appearance of treacle. Modern waterproof grease is often white and is much thinner, allowing bearings to move more freely and giving longer protection.

The bottom bracket unit will need repacking with grease most often, at least once a year, but more often if the bike has consistently been ridden in the wet.

Hubs will also need re-greasing, but should last slightly longer than the bottom bracket.

Headsets and pedals, the other areas where bearings are fitted, should last considerably longer. If top quality headsets and pedals are used, they may never need attention and the only time that these components are removed from the bicycle is for replacement.

An advantage with many new components, especially those for mountain bikes, is that they are fitted with water seals between the bearing face and the axles. This keeps the water and dirt out and the grease in.

Also use waterproof grease for cables. When new cables are fitted, or should the old cables become stiff, a liberal coating of the grease along the inner wire will help it slide easily through the outer casing.

Another application for the grease is on the seat pillar and the handlebar stem to prevent a bonding reaction between the alloy of the components and the steel frame tubing. A small amount of the lubricant smeared around the stem and the seat pillar will save them being ruined when they have to be cut out of the frame. The grease also allows for easier handlebar and saddle height adjustment.

A small quantity of grease inside the stem will also prevent the coned-shaped wedge of the expander bolt from jamming.

Tools

Even if you have no interest whatever in maintenance you will need at least basic tools to carry out routine and emergency repairs.

Thankfully, cycle components have become standardized and metric sizes are used for most nuts and allen key(US:hexagon wrench) bolts, making the range of tools smaller.

It would be impossible to adjust your position without five and six-millimetre allen keys as these are needed to alter the handlebar and seat pillar heights. The five-millimetre size is the most popular of all. This not only fits the majority of seat bolts, but is also needed for the chainring fixing bolts, gear cable fixing bolts, allen-key brake anchorage bolts and cable bolts, plus handlebar bolts on some stems.

For what the five-millimetre allen key does not fit, you will need the six-millimetre size. The stem bolt, which fits in the frame, is the main use for this key, but the bolt which secures the rear gear mechanism to the frame is another. Some manufacturers use this larger size for the same applications as the five millimetre.

Although more manufacturers are moving towards allen-key fittings, you will still find several conventional nuts on your bike, including the gear mechanisms and the brakes. You need open ended spanners(US:wrenches), available with different sizes at each end.
An eight and nine-millimetre combination, plus a 10 and 11-millimetre spanner will solve most of your gear and brake problems.

Avoid adjustable spanners for these small sizes. It is difficult to get a tight fit and the nuts will soon become rounded. Multi-spanners are not a good idea either. These may seem a good, cheaper alternative, but with up to eight sizes on one spanner, they are bulky and difficult to use.

Add small screwdrivers, both Phillips and conventional fitting, a small pair of pliers, plus three tyre levers(US:tire irons) and you will have a basic tool set. However, these tools will only allow you to do the minimum of basic work and as you become more experienced, you will soon demand more.

The next stage of tooling allows the simple removal, replacement and adjustment of components. You will need three more double-ended metric spanners, 12 and 13, 14 and 15, plus 16 and 17-millimetre combinations. These will enable you to do more elaborate tasks, such as fitting and removing pedals and when used in conjunction with an extractor tool, the removal of the chainset or left crank.

In addition to the extractor it will also be necessary to purchase a bottom bracket crank-nut spanner. This has a recessed fitting to extend inside the crank arm.

Having removed the chainset you then need the special tools to remove or adjust the bottom bracket axle. Two large spanners are required and these will cost you only slightly less than a new set of tyres. The investment is worth it as they are high quality tools, with one featuring two pins which locate in the adjustable bottom bracket cup and the other has a half-round section which fits around the locking ring. Their size gives them the necessary leverage.

It is also a double investment, as these – like many cycle spanners – are double-ended. Your pair of bottom bracket tools should also have two large spanners which fit the headset, another component that will need adjusting.

Do not try to use an large adjustable spanner for the headset locking nut, as with the considerable leverage required, it will round over the spanner flats and only a custom-made spanner is thin enough to fit on to the adjustable headset bearing race.

Other tools for simple adjustments are a set of thin cone spanners. As with the metric spanners these are supplied in two-size combinations, in

Tools

1.	11–15 millimetre spanners (US: wrenches)
2.	Peg spanner and headset
3.	Lockring spanner and headset
4.	Fixed-cup spanner
5.	Cone spanners
6.	Chainset spanner
7.	Chainset remover
8.	Chain link tool
9.	Cable cutters
10.	Spoke key
11.	Allen keys (US: hexagon wrenches)
12.	Block remover (US: Freewheel cluster remover)
13.	T-bar spanner (US: T-bar socket wrench)
14.	Tyre levers (US: Tire irons)
15.	Pliers
16.	Screwdrivers
17.	Puncture repair kit (US: Tube patch kit)
18.	File

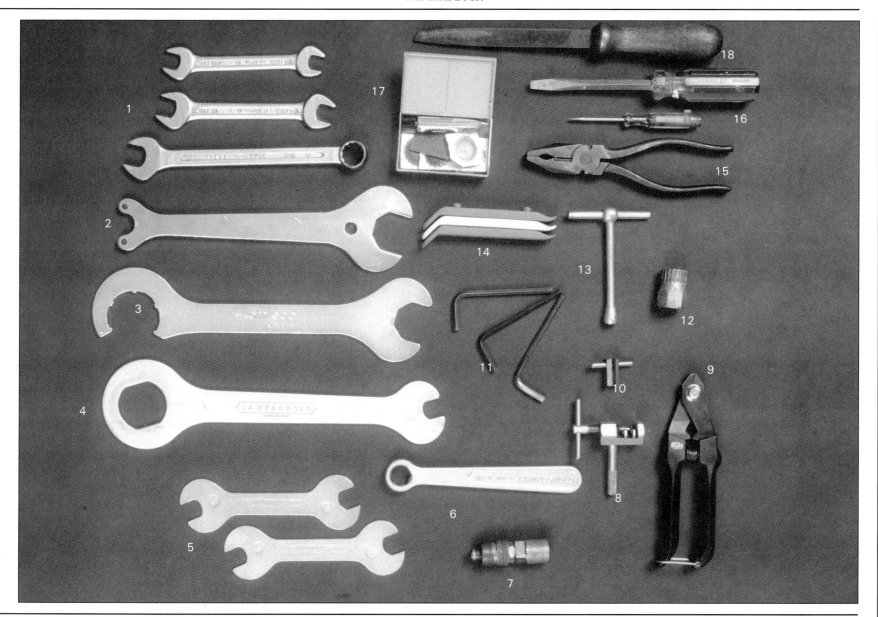

13 and 14 or 15 and 16-millimetre sizes. The metric spanners(US:wrenches) in these same sizes will be used in conjunction with the cone spanners to remove and tighten the lock nuts.

Cone spanners are now also required for the centering adjustment of many types of side-pull brake stirrups. Conventional spanners are too thick to fit on to the brake spindle.

To complete this second-stage tool set, a chain rivet extractor for fitting and removing chains or removing tight links, plus a pair of good quality cable cutters are essential. The cable cutters are needed as all cables are over-sized and need cutting to length. As cycle cables are hardened, top-quality cutters are essential as cheaper versions soon become blunt and will fray the cable ends.

Many riders never need or bother to buy any further tooling. The rest is up to you. You can turn your garage into a replica of your local cycle shop, or you can leave the more involved jobs to the professionals.

It will be necessary at some stage to replace both bottom bracket cups, but at this stage you only have tools for adjusting and removing the adjustable side. This is enough for re-greasing the unit, but the left-hand cup will eventually wear out and another heavy duty spanner is necessary.

This ring spanner will not slip as it makes perfect contact with the bottom bracket cup. Again do not use an adjustable spanner for the usual reasons.

If the bike is dismantled, some resort to grip-

A cyclist's double-ended screwdriver is ideal for adjustment.

A Shimano crank extractor. Shimano equipment is common on many of today's bikes.

ping the cup in a vice and turning the frame. Be warned, this is one of the easiest ways to chip the frame and it is also very difficult to fit a new cup in this way.

Once you have the basics, extra tools can only make the job easier, and it would be worth considering a cycle workshop stand. These can be expensive, but as a guide the simplest are usually the best. A device which fits on the chain and seat stays to hold the rear wheel off the ground, allows all manner of work to be completed on the transmission and prevents the bike from falling over.

Workshop stands which lift both wheels off the ground, supporting the machine under the bottom bracket and cramping to the down tube, make bottom bracket and headset work much easier.

A special tool often called a 'third hand' is great for brake adjustment. It is an inexpensive item which fits through the spokes to grip the brake blocks together to make cable adjustment perfect every time.

Although a simple spoke key would be useful for emergency spoke replacement, it is best to leave wheel repairs to the experts. Wheel truing stands are a waste of money unless you know exactly what you are doing and wheel building skills cannot be learnt overnight.

Special extractors are needed to remove free-wheels from the rear hubs. Although these units are not very expensive, the act of removing the freewheel requires considerable effort. If you are buying a replacement freewheel, take the complete wheel to your cycle shop; it will not be expensive to have them replace it. This is an operation which is not repeated very often, except by top racing cyclists.

If you decide you need to change your gear ratios regularly, you would do better with two pairs of wheels to make the operation simpler.

Spoke repairs

1 Spokes normally break where they join the hub, so you will need to remove the spoke head and then unwind the nipple from the rim.

2 Push the new spoke through the hub, either outwards or inwards to replace the broken one.

3 Feed the new spoke back through the rim taking care to bend it as little as possible.

4 Re-tighten the spoke and spin the wheel to see if it needs re-trueing.

5 Beware of spokes which are too long. Use a small file to remove any surplus which protrudes above nipple.

Tyre repair *(US:tire repair)*

A racing cyclist replacing a tubular tyre. He is using a specially powerful adhesive to ensure that the tyre does not come off the rim. (Right) Changing a tyre on a mountain bike.

1 Carefully insert one tyre lever(US:tire iron) under the bead of the tyre and run another lever around the circumference to remove it from the rim.

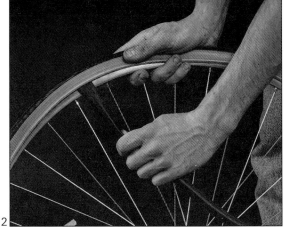

2 Great care should be taken not to pinch the inner tube and damage it further. It can now be pulled from the tyre working in both directions towards the valve.

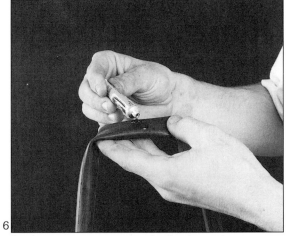

6 Apply a generous amount of adhesive to the puncture area and then allow this to partially dry.

3 Lift the valve out of its hole in the rim to remove the inner tube and run your fingers inside the tyre to find and remove the cause of the puncture. The object will be sharp so be very careful not to cut yourself.

4 Partly inflate the inner tube so that you can locate the puncture.

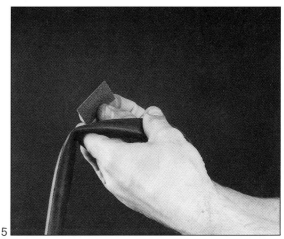

5 Buff the area of the puncture with a light sandpaper to give the best possible adhesion for the repair patch.

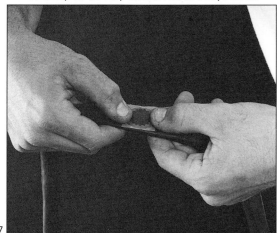

7 Push the puncture repair patch into position and hold firmly for several minutes.

8 Wait for the patch to dry and then slightly inflate the inner tube and push the valve into the hole in the rim.

9 Gradually feed the inner tube back under the tyre as it is fitted back on to the rim. Be careful not to pinch the tube. Once you are satisfied the tyre is firmly in place on the rim, inflate the tube to riding pressure.

Bearing adjustment

There are three main bearing groups on a bike which will need adjusting at least once a year, the bottom bracket, the headset and the hubs.

The quality of these components determines how often they need attention. The best equipment is designed to take more punishment, whereas less expensive components will need repair and adjustment much sooner. This is especially true of hubs with lower-priced component sets which often leave the factory adjusted too tight and need to be slackened off to prevent excessive wear of the cones and bearings.

With quick-release hubs it is important to remember that there should always be a slight amount of play on the axle as the quick-release mechanism further compresses the cones when it is locked closed.

The most frequent bearing adjustment is the tightening of the bottom bracket, headset and hubs which gradually become loose with wear.

A loose headset will judder when braking and a bottom bracket axle or rear hub bearing with excessive play gives a knocking noise under load.

Pedal bearings are difficult to adjust on all but the most expensive models, but thankfully such adjustment is not normally necessary. To tighten or loosen the cone lock nut normally requires a metric socket spanner(US:wrench) between 10 and 13 millimetres.

The most important point about correctly adjusted bearings is that they give longer wear and improved performance. Cycling can be

BOTTOM BRACKETS

HEADSETS

PEDALS

HUBS

tough enough at times without making things harder for yourself.

For headset adjustment you will need two large flat spanners. These double ended spanners will often also include the two-pin tool and the half round spanner necessary for bottom bracket adjustment. You will also need a crank nut socket spanner and crank extractor tool.

The cones require two flat cone spanners and for the lock nuts standard metric spanners are often handy.

BOTTOM BRACKETS

To adjust the bottom bracket axle remove the crank fixing bolt and then fit the extractor tool to take off the crank.

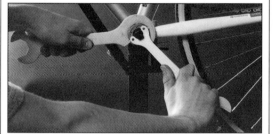

With crank removed fit two-pin tool in adjustable cup and slacken off nut with spanner Adjust, then re-tighten bottom bracket.

HEADSETS

Holding the adjustable race in place with the spanner(US:wrench), use the other headset spanner to slacken off the lock nut.

Set the adjustable race so that the headset spins easily, but there is no play and then hold it in place and re-tighten the lock nut.

PEDALS

Remove the pedal dust cap with the appropriate metric spanner.

Check for sideways movement to see if the pedal bearings are too loose. If the pedal does not spin easily, then the bearings are too tight.

1

HUBS Hold the adjustable cone with one spanner and use another cone spanner to release the lock nut.

2

Grip the opposite side of the axle with a metric spanner and adjust the cones so that there is only a very slight amount of play in the bearings.

3

Keep the adjustable cone in the required position and tighten down the lock nut.

Brake adjustment

Brake adjustment is probably the most regular maintenance you will carry out and it is also the most important. Reduced braking efficiency can be lethal, so the importance of correctly adjusted brakes cannot be over-emphasized.

As the brake blocks wear down the cables will need tightening to compensate for the increased gap between the blocks and rims. Most stirrups are equipped with adjusters which will take up much of the slack caused by block wear. The cables will also stretch slightly and at least once a year it will be necessary to turn the adjuster down, release the cable fastening bolt and take in the slack cable.

Take care that you have securely tightened the cable fixing bolts.

Also inspect the stirrups to make certain that the brake blocks are coming into contact squarely with the rims. Too high and they will damage to the side walls of the tyre(US:tire), too low and they risk going into the spokes.

When checking brake block alignment also examine the blocks for small stones which may be lodged in the tread as these will score and damage the rims if they are not removed.

Brake stirrups may also need centering occasionally. Until recently this was a problem, but now almost all side-pull stirrups are equipped with spanner flats on the spindle. A twist of a cone spanner will soon have both blocks an equal distance from the rim.

For brake adjustment you will need five- and six millimetre allen keys(US: hexagon wrenches), eight and nine plus 10- and 11-millimetre open ended spanner(US: wrench) combinations, and a cone spanner for brake centering.

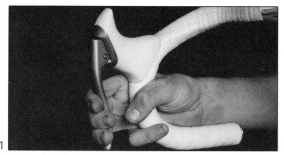

1 If your brakes are adjusted too tight as shown by this lever, then the brake blocks will rub against the rim.

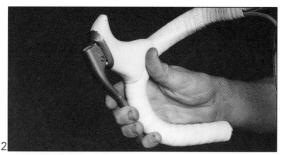

2 Brakes which have too much slack will, in exaggerated cases, have the lever come into contact with the handlebars before the blocks meet the rim.

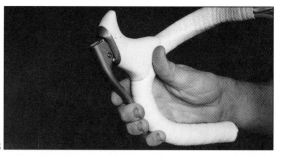

3 Adjust the stirrups with the cable fastening bolt. Hold the brake blocks together to pull the right amount of cable through.

4 For exact brake adjustment use the small adjusters on the brake stirrups. These should also be used to compensate for brake block wear.

5 If the brake stirrups are not centered, then one brake block will rub on the rim. Use a cone spanner to fit the spanner flats on the brake spindle.

6 Brake blocks must be parallel with the rim for the best possible braking performance. A brake block which is too low could go in to the spokes.

7 A brake block which is adjusted too high is just as dangerous and the blocks will wear away the side walls of the tyre to cause a blow-out.

8 Grip the brake stirrups together to bring the brake blocks into contact with the rim and use an allen key to adjust the blocks to the correct height.

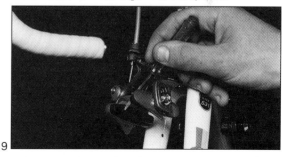

9 Using a small screwdriver check the grooves in the brake block pattern for any small stones which will score and damage the rims.

Gear adjustment

If your gearing system is correctly set-up, then you will hardly ever have to adjust it. Every time you ride·your bike you are testing the system so problems soon become obvious.

Most bikes are now equipped with an index 'click-into-gear' system and any trouble with gear changes usually comes from the cable slipping through the fixing bolts. Many rear mechanisms have an adjuster to compensate for stretch in the cable.

The most effective index system has the tautest possible cable which allows perfect gear changes. Gradually allow more slack until the rear gear mechanism changes perfectly. If the cable is too tight it pulls the mechanism away from its pre-set position.

Check that the rear gear mechanism does not go too close to the spokes in bottom gear and that it is not in danger of jamming between the smallest sprocket and the axle in top gear.

Many riders experience trouble with the chain coming off the big chainring when changing up, or falling off the small chainring when changing down. Check that the front changer is close enough to the chainset, it should be approximately five millimetres above the large chainring and should be parallel to the chainset. Adjust the inner setting in bottom gear in the small chainring and the outer setting in the big chainring and the top sprocket.

For gear adjustment, you need five- and six-millimetre allen keys(US:hexagon wrenches), 8 and 9 plus 10- and 11-millimetre open-ended spanner combinations and pliers.

1 Adjust the gear cable tension so that it is neither too tight nor too slack. If the cable is too tight the index system will not work properly.

2 Shift to the smallest sprocket and large chainring and adjust for top gear. Do not slacken the screw too much as chain will jam between axle and rear end.

3 Select the small chainring and largest sprocket for bottom gear adjustment. Take great care not to allow the mechanism to go too close to the spokes.

4 The small screw on the top pivot of the gear mechanism should be tightened to increase the angle of the unit if larger sprockets are to be used, and loosened if smaller ratios are chosen.

5 Set the height of the front changer approximately five millimetres above the chainring. With elliptical chainrings, such as Shimano Biopace, set the changer at the highest point of the ring.

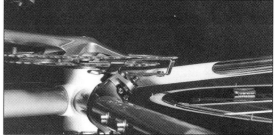

6 For positive gear changes it is important to get the angle of the front changer correct. The mechanism should always be set parallel with the outer chainring.

7 Slacken the cable fixing bolt on the front mechanism and pull cable tight with a pair of pliers before re-tightening the bolt with an allen key (US: hexagon wrench).

8 Select the bottom sprocket and small chainring to adjust the inner movement of the front changer. The back of the mechanism cage should just clear the chain in this position.

9 To set the outer movement of the front changer you need to be on the large chainring and the top sprocket. The chain should just clear the front of the cage and should not foul the crank.

Bearing service and replacement

With a normal amount of riding, bearing service and replacement should not be needed more than twice a year. It is not just the quantity of miles, but also the quality, as mountain bikes ridden over very wet and muddy terrain will need stripping down more often.

The three areas which will require your attention are the bottom bracket, headset and hubs and these will need greasing and inspecting for wear. You will need to look at the bottom bracket axle, the bracket cups, the bearings surfaces inside the hubs, the cones, plus all four headset races. If you are in any doubt about the quality of the bearings, then you should replace them.

Do not worry too much about pedals. With less expensive models the actual pedal body will often be worn out before the bearing needs attention. Good quality pedals have superior bearings which rarely need adjusting.

As bearing surfaces get worn they become shiny and eventually pitted. Badly worn bearing surfaces make proper adjustment impossible and the rider must compromise by having bearings either too loose or too tight.

Considerable tooling is required. For the bottom bracket you will need the two-pin tool and the half-round spanner for the adjustable cup, plus the large ring spanner for the fixed cup.

To remove the chainset you will need the crank nut socket spanner and an extractor tool, plus a small screwdriver to remove the crank dust cap.

HEADSETS

CHAINSETS

HUBS

PEDALS

Tools for bearing service and replacement

● For the headset you require the two special large open-ended spanners and a six-millimetre allen key to remove the handlebar stem.

Hubs require 13 and 14 plus 15 and 16-millimetre cone spanner combinations. Standard metric spanners in the same sizes are handy for some lock nuts.

Socket spanners between 10 and 13-millimetres are normally required to fit the lock nuts on the pedal bearings.

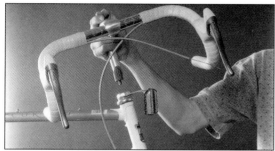

1 To service the headset remove the stem by loosening the allen key fixing bolt. A light tap with a hammer will release the wedge-shape nut from the frame.

2 Release the headset lock nut gripping it with the correct spanner, while holding the adjusting race in place with another headset tool.

3 Once the adjusting race of the headset has been removed the fork column can be released from the frame.

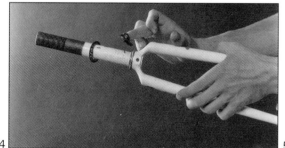

4 Pack grease around the fork column race of the headset. Keep the bearing cage around the column.

5 More grease is needed up inside the bottom headset race. A waterproof grease is the best choice.

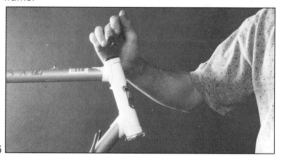

6 Follow the same greasing procedure with the top race of the headset. Do not be over generous with the lubricant.

7 The bearing cage is placed in the adjusting race and wiped with grease to keep it in position.

8 Hold the adjusting race in position on the top race and screw the fork column up and into place.

9 Using the two special headset spanners set the adjusting race and then hold it in position while the lock nut is tightened down.

BEARING SERVICE AND REPLACEMENT

CHAINSETS

1
Use a small screwdriver to prise off the dust cap from the crank. Other dust caps may have a screw-in design.

2
A bottom bracket socket spanner(US:wrench) is used to remove the chainset fixing bolt from the crank.

3
The extractor tool is screwed into place, tightened and then the bolt is screwed home to release the chainset.

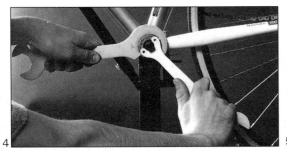

4
Once the other crank has been removed the adjusting cup should be held in place while the lock ring is removed.

5
Using the large two-pin spanner the adjusting cup can now be unscrewed from the frame.

6
Remove the adjusting cup and pull the bottom bracket axle complete with bearings out of the frame.

7
With the large ring spanner remove the fixed cup, but remember this usually has an anti-clockwise, left-hand thread.

8
Replace the fixed cup with greased bearing race, insert the axle and then screw the adjustable cup into position and fasten it with the lock ring.

9
Bolt on both sides of the chainset with the special socket spanner and replace the dust caps.

THE BIKE BOOK

1 Use a thin cone spanner(US:wrench) to hold the cone nut in place and another metric spanner to release the lock nut.

2 With one side of the spindle removed the axle can be taken out of the hub. Take care not to lose the bearings.

3 Pack the bearings with grease in the hub shell and the replace the axle.

HUBS

4 Hold the locked-up end of the axle with a spanner and tighten the cone into position.

5 With a cone spanner holding the cone nut in position tighten the lock nut down onto it with another spanner.

PEDALS

Remove the dust cap at the end of the pedal axle with the relevant metric spanner.

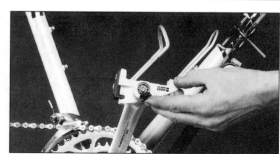

Repack the pedal bearing with grease and the replace the dust cap to keep out water and dirt.

BEARING SERVICE AND REPLACEMENT

Brake service and replacement

There are two main areas for concern with the brakes, the brake blocks and the cables. Both are subject to wear, with the blocks taking a considerable pounding, especially in gritty winter conditions.

Years ago riders would remove the blocks from the brake shoes to replace them, but today many brakes feature moulded blocks which incorporate the brake shoe, making replacement much easier.

Brake blocks normally feature a design to disperse water when they come into contact with the rim. If the blocks become too worn, then this advantage is lost.

Brake cables will stretch and may eventually fray. Frayed cables must be replaced at once because they are substantially weakened and can jam inside the outer casing.

Also check the outer casing for any cracks or breaks. These too can cause the cable to jam.

For cantilever brakes, as used on mountain bikes, and for centre-pull brakes there is an extra straddle wire to inspect.

The only other damage which is usual with side-pull brakes is that the upper arm of the caliper can be bent it if is smashed against the frame in a crash.

Brake levers should always be securely fastened to the handlebars and the allen key (US: hexagon wrench) fixng bolts inside the levers should be checked periodically.

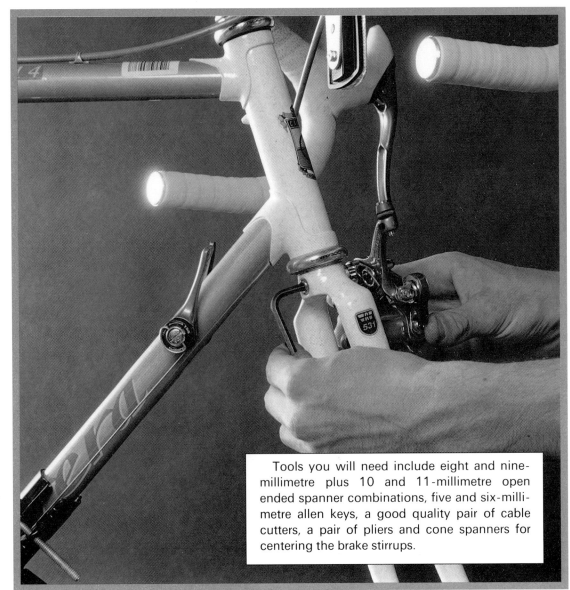

Tools you will need include eight and nine-millimetre plus 10 and 11-millimetre open ended spanner combinations, five and six-millimetre allen keys, a good quality pair of cable cutters, a pair of pliers and cone spanners for centering the brake stirrups.

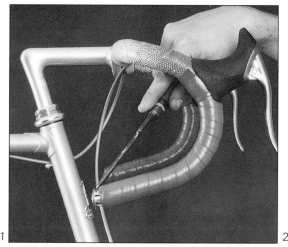

1

Prise out the handlebar end stops with a screwdriver. Other types of end stop may be the screw-in variety.

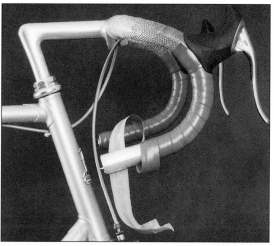

2

Unwind the handlebar tape. If you are careful there is no need to rip it and it can be used again.

3

Release the brake cable by loosening the allen key fastening bolt on the brake stirrup.

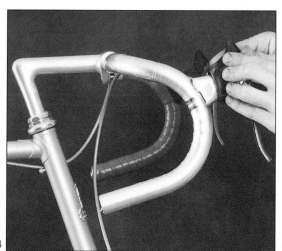

4

Pull back the brake lever hood rubbers. This will help to release and re-fit the cables as well as removing the levers from the handlebars.

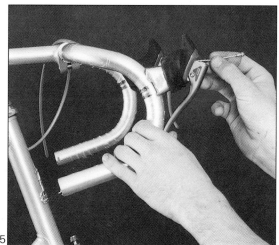

5

Pull inner brake cable out through brake lever hood.

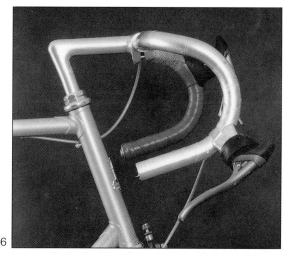

6

Loosen the brake lever fixing bolt and twist and pull the levers off the handlebars.

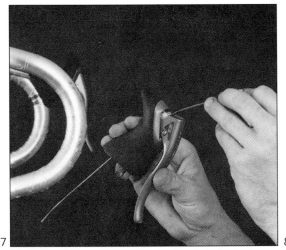

7 Fit a new brake cable inner wire through the brake lever.

8 Twist and pull the brake lever back into position on the handlebars.

9 Use a straight edge to check that the brake levers are level and then fasten in position.

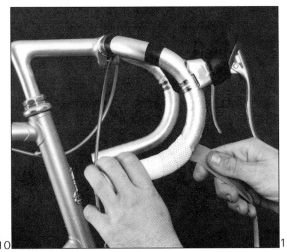

10 Re-tape the handlebars starting from the end plugs. Finish just before the stem and secure with insulating tape.

11 The brake inner cable should be greased and fitted into the outer casing before being reconnected to the stirrup.

12 Use the adjuster on the brake stirrup for perfect braking performance.

Gear servicing and replacement

Gear servicing is relatively simple, consisting mainly of the maintenance of the twin gear cables and of the rollers on the rear mechanism.

As with brake cables, the gear wires should be checked for any signs of fraying. Where the cable passes through covered cable, as it does between the chainstay and the rear mechanism, it should be lubricated with grease. The gear wire guides under the bottom bracket shell should also be inspected to check that there are no blockages which may jam the cable.

The rollers on the rear gear mechanism are not normally mounted on ball bearings, but have metal sleeves inserted in the plastic rollers to rotate on. This is a satisfactory arrangement except for when the rollers get soaked in water or covered in mud, after which they are prone to making a loud squeaking noise until they are lubricated.

An occasional squirt with a lubrication spray will suffice, or the rollers can be dismantled and packed with a waterproof grease for a longer lasting solution to this problem.

Check all fastening bolts, the large allen-key bolt which fixes the rear gear mechanism to the frame and the allen key bolt which secures the clip holding the front changer in position.

Only simple tooling is required for this service work. You will need five and six-millimetre allen keys (US: hexagon wrench), eight- and nine-millimetre and 10- and 11-millimetre open-ended spanner(US:wrench) combinations, a pair of pliers, plus good-quality cable cutters.

GEAR SERVICING AND REPLACEMENT

1 Loosen the gear cable fastening bolts on the front changer and the rear gear mechanism.

2 Remove the cable from the rear gear mechanism and slide off the outer casing.

3 Carefully pull the gear cable through the gear cable stop on the chainstays.

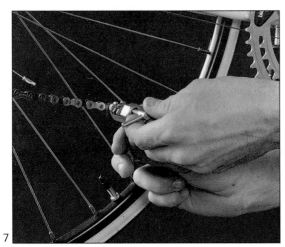

7 Insert the chain into the rivet extractor and wind the screw down onto the chain to push out the rivet.

8 You only need to push the rivet as far as the back plate to remove the chain from the bike.

9 Carefully feed the chain out from the bike over the chainset.

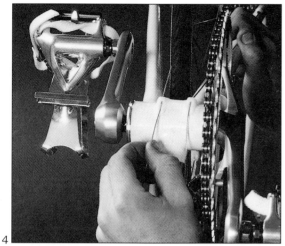

4 The cables will need easing through certain areas including the cable guides under the bottom bracket.

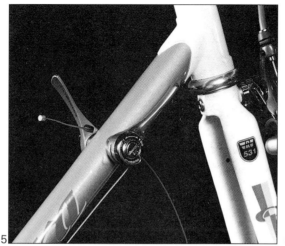

5 Finally the gear cables can be pulled out from the levers.

6 Replace the cables feeding them back along the same route, greasing the areas which go inside covered cable and then re-tighten the fixing bolts.

10 Help the chain through the roller cage of the rear gear mechanism.

11 Replace the chain reversing the removal procedure and use the extractor to push the rivet back into place.

12 Check the chain for stiff links. Look at where the chain jumps on the sprockets and then locate the problem area by hand.

Fitting the mudguards
(US:fenders)

1

With a spanner(US:wrench) undo and remove the mudguard(US:fender) at the back of the brakes. Most mudguards are made of plastic.

2

Slide the mudguard underneath the brakes and the brake bridge. Older cycles may have steel mudguards.

3

Carefully squeeze the clip with a pair of pliers under the mudguard to prevent movement.

4

Tighten up the nut and bolt to the mudguard stay.

5

Position nut and bolt onto the mudguard and then thread the nut, making sure that the stay hole is on the outside of the mudguard.

6 Clip the mudguard to the frame. Make sure that the mudguard is completely fast and that it cannot slip off.

7 Place the clip over the mudguard and then push over the bolt on the brakes.

8 With a spanner now tighten up the nut onto the back of the brake bridge.

9 Using a small screwdriver and spanner fix the nut and bolt to the stay and to the frame. Be sure the bolt does not foul the spokes.

10 With a spanner tighten the nuts on the mudguard stay. Be sure that the tyre(US:tire) does not rub against the mudguard.

11 Fix protective ends over the mudguard stays to prevent accidental snagging against any clothing.

Useful Organizations

Leisure cycling/ Cycle touring

Belgium
Touring Club Royal de Belgique (TCB)
Rue de la Loi 44
B-1040 Bruxelles

Denmark
Dansk Cyklist Forbund (DCF)
Kjeld Landges Gade 14
DK-1367 Copenhagen K

France
Fédération Française de Cyclotourisme (FFCT)
8 rue Jean-Marie Jego
F-75013 Paris

German Federal Republic
Allgemeiner Deutscher Fahrrad-Club (ADFC)
Am Dobben 91
D-2800 Bremen 1

Luxembourg
Union Luxembourgeoise de Cyclotouristes
39 rue de l'Etoile
F-57190 Florange
France

Netherlands
Koninklijke Nederlandse Toeristenbond
(ANWB)
Wassenaarseweg 220
Postbus 93200
NL-2509 BA Den Haag

Nederlandse Rijwiel Toer Unie (NRTU)
Postbus 326
NL-3900 AH Veenendaal

Republic of Ireland
An Oige
39 Mountjoy Square
Dublin 1
(*the Republic's youth hostels organization*)

Switzerland
Touring Club Suisse (TCS)
Section Cyclotourisme
9 rue Pierre-Fatio
CH-1200 Geneva

United Kingdom
Cyclists' Touring Club (CTC)
69 Meadrow
Godalming
Surrey
GU7 3HS

Youth Hostels Association (YHA)
8 St Stephen's Hill
St Albans
Herts
AL1 2DY (*covers England and Wales only*)

Scottish Youth Hostels Association (SYHA)
7 Glebe Crescent
Stirling FK8 2JA

Youth Hostels Association of Northern Ireland
(YHANI)
56 Bradbury Place
Belfast

United States
Bikecentennial
PO Box 8308
Missoula
MT 59807

League of American Wheelmen (LAW)
Suite 209
6707 Whitestone Road
Baltimore
MD 21207

Cycling Sport

Audax UK
Ray Haswell
22b, Kings Avenue
Lower Parkestone
POOLE
Dorset BH14 9OG

Audax USA
International Randonneurs
Audax Correspondent
Konski Engineers PC
727, North Salina Street
SYRACUSE NY 13208

Road racing

In order to race on the road, you need to join a cycling club. Write to your national governing body and they will send you details of clubs in your area. The racing secretary of the club you join will be able to give you full details of racing in that area. If you want to race abroad, you should contact your national body before going: they will be able to inform you of any special requirements you will need in the country in which you intend racing.

British Cycling Federation
36, Rockingham Road
KETTERING
Northants NN16 8AG

Fédération Française de Cyclisme
43, Rue de Dunkerque
75480 PARIS
Cedex 10
France

Federazione Ciclistica Italiana
Via Leopoldo Franchetti 2
00194 ROME
Italy

Ligue Vélocipedique Belge
49, Avenue du Globe
1190 BRUSSELS
Belgium

Koninlijke Nederlandsche Wielren Unie
Postbus 136
Polanerbaan 15
3447 GN WOERDEN
Holland

US Cycling Federation
1750, East Boulder Street
COLORADO SPRINGS
Colorado 80909
USA

Time-trialling

Again, club membership, though not essential, is highly desirable. Contact your National Federation for club details as described above.

Cyclo-Cross

Britain:
Contact either National Federation or British Cyclo-Cross Association
Mrs Joan Edwards
59 Jordan Road
SUTTON COLDFIELD
West Midlands, B75 5AE

Mountain-bike Racing

Britain:
Mountain-Bike Club
Santon House
SANTON DOWNHAM
Suffolk IP27 0TT

USA:
Contact National Federation

Human Powered Vehicles

Britain:
HPV Club
John Kingsbury
22, Oakfield Road
BOURNE END
Bucks, SL5 5QR

USA:
IHPVA
PO Box 51255
INDIANAPOLIS
Indianapolis
USA

Triathlon

Britain:
Ken Wood
9, Lea Springs
FLEET
Hampshire GU13 8AR

USA:
Contact National Federation

Books

(1) General

Badminton Library of Sports and Pastimes: Cycling, ed Viscount Bury and G. Lacy Hillier (Longmans Green, various editions from 1887, long out of print)

Bicycling Across America, Robert Winning (Wilderness Press, 1988, ISBN 0 89997 092 3)

Bicycling Science, Frank R. Whitt and David G. Wilson (MIT Press), 1982, ISBN 0262 23111 5)

Bicycling the Pacific Coast, Tim Kirkendall and Vicky Spring (The Mountaineers, Seattle, 1988, ISBN 089886 081 4)

Cycle Tourer's Handbook, Tim Hughes (Batsford, 1987, ISBN 0 7134 5136 X)

Cycling in Europe, Nick Crane (Oxford Illustrated Press, 1984, ISBN 0 902280 77 5)

Cycling Off-road and the Law, Neil Horton (Cyclists' Touring Club (CTC), 1987, no ISBN)

Cyclist's Britain, ed Andrew Duncan and Mel Petersen (Pan/Ordnance Survey, 1985, ISBN 0 330 28610)

Follow the Map: the Ordnance Survey Guide, John G. Wilson (A&C Black, 1985, 07136 2459 0)

Great Cycle Tours of Britain, Tim Hughes (Ward Lock, 1988, ISBN 0 7063 6597 6)

Penguin Book of the Bicycle, Roderick Watson and Martin Gray (Penguin, 1978, 0 14 004297 0)

Richard's Mountain Bike Book, Charles Kelly and Nick Crane (Oxford Illustrated Press, 1988)

Richard's New Bicycle Book, Richard Ballantine (Oxford Illustrated Press, 1989)

(2) Cycle Sport

Alpaca to Swimsuit, Bernard Thompson
(Geerings of Ashford, 1988)

Hearts of Lions, Peter Nye (W.W. Norton
and Co, 1988)

Kings of the Road, Robin Magowan and
Graham Watson (Springfield Books, 1987)

*The Macmillan Dictionary of Sports and
Games,* J.A. Cuden (The Macmillan Press,
1980)

Mountain Biking, Max Glaskin and Jeremy
Torr (Pelham Books, 1988)

Swim + Bike + Run, Aleck Hunter and Eric
Kirschbaum (George Allen and Unwin,
1985)

Cycling Weekly Magazine

New Cyclist Magazine

Winning Magazine

157

Index

Acknowledgements

We would particularly like to thank R.J. Chicken & Son Ltd for kindly supplying photographic material and Halfords for the loan of bikes. We also thank *Freewheeel, Cycling Weekly* and *Winning* for photographs.

   We acknowledge with thanks the following picture sources:
Alesa: page 18 (right)
Nick Burrows Engineering pages 29 (bottom right), 121 (left),
R.J. Chicken & Sons Ltd: pages 37 (left), 41 (centre)
Stuart Clarke: 70, 115
Cycling Weekly: pages 65, 68, 69
Dawes Cycles Ltd: pages 20 (bottom), 21
Duegi (Italy): pages 36, 37 (centre)
Freewheel: pages 22 (centre below), 53, 56, 57, 60 (centre)
Halfords: pages 26, 28, 62
Hella Ltd: page 40
Tim Hughes: pages 8, 9, 10, 11, 16 (centre), 20 (top right), 38, 39, 44, 45, 46, 47, 49, 51, 52, 54, 55, 58, 59, 66, 196
Illustrated London News: page 12 (bottom right)
Peter Knottley: page 67
George Longstaff: page 29, (left and top right)
Muddy Fox: pages 22 (right), 22 (top left)
Photosport International: pages 12, 13 (extreme left, extreme right), 24 (top left), 41 (centre top), 60 (right), 63, 64, 71, 73, 75, 76, 77, 78, 79, 82, 83, 84, 85, 86, 87, 88, 89, 90, 91, 92, 93, 94, 95, 96, 97, 98, 100, 102, 103, 104, 105, 106, 113, 134, 157
Raleigh Industries Ltd: pages 20, 23, 25
Sella Italia (Italy); pages 34, 35
Spaarnestad Fotoarchieff (Holland): pages 69, 80, 81
Sachs Maillard: pages 16 (right), 17
Bernard Thompson: pages, 114, 116, 119, 120, 121
Colin Underhill: pages 108, 109, 110, 111
Vredestein (Holland): pages 18 (left), 19, 41 (centre below), 65 (centre), 72
Graham Watson/*Triathlete Magazine:* page 121 (right)
Winning: page 118
David Worthy: pages 122-133, 135-155